Journey of the Heart

Journey of the Heart

A Way of Praying on the Gospels

Thomas S. Kane

ST. BEDE'S PUBLICATIONS
Still River, Massachusetts

Nihil Obstat:

Rev. John A. Alesandro, S.T.L., J.C.D.
  Censor Librorum
  October 22, 1979

Imprimatur:

Most Reverend John R. McGann, D.D.
  Bishop of Rockville Center
  October 24, 1979

The Nihil obstat and Imprimatur are official declarations
that the manuscript is free of doctrinal or moral error.

Acknowledgement:

Bible quotes from the Revised Standard Version of the Bible,
copyrighted 1946, 1952 © 1971, 1973.

LIBRARY OF CONGRESS CATALOGING IN PUBLICATION DATA

Kane, Thomas S., 1942-
  Journey of the heart.

  1. Prayer.   2. Bible. N.T. Gospels—Criticism, interpre-
tation, etc.   I. Title.
BV210.2.K33   242'.5   81-5278
ISBN 0-932506-13-5   AACR2

Contents

For my dear family,
who have always been for me
images of faith and fidelity

Foreword

During the first thousand years in which Christian Fathers wrote about the ways of prayer, from Evagrius Ponticus in the fourth century to the dominating influence of scholasticism in the fourteenth, one of the favored means for summing up teaching on prayer was to employ four words: *lectio, meditatio, oratio,* and *contemplatio.* A literal English translation of these four words—reading, meditation, prayer, and contemplation—does not adequately convey their significance in this context. *Lectio,* or *lectio divina* as the more common usage would have it, includes far more than reading.

Back in a period when most people could not read, the term rather connoted *receiving the divine word,* whether through personal reading, hearing the word read in the liturgical assembly, receiving it from a spiritual father, recalling it from one's own memory, seeing it depicted in fresco, icon or stained glass, acted out in the mystery play, or existentially expressed in creation—the sky, the land, the water, the bird, the tree. *Lectio* is a quiet receptive openness to hearing God speak through whatever media are aptly at hand. It is to receive the word of life.

Meditatio is allowing the word to come to life in us. More often in those early days it involved the repetition—mentally or with the lips—of a phrase of Scripture, repeated over and over again until it formed the heart. The Fathers liked to use the example of the "clean animal": The cow goes out to the pasture and eats the fresh green clover (*lectio*), then it retires to the shade of a great oak, settles down, and regurgitates what it has collected, to chew it over and over (*meditatio*) till there is extracted from it the makings of rich, creamy milk (*oratio*). Through meditation a rational assent to the realities of divine presence and revelation is changed into a real assent, to use Cardinal Newman's happy distinction. We hear the word of God, and in faith, assent to it: "Yes, that is true." But through *meditatio*, the word forms our heart and being, it comes alive in us. Our whole being says, "Yes, that's it,"—a real assent.

When the word calls forth such a response from us, we are in prayer—*oratio*. Prayer always begins with God. He speaks first. He speaks the creation. He speaks each one of us into being. He speaks to us, revealing himself and his plan of love. When we truly hear—*lectio* and *meditatio*—it is time to respond—*oratio*. According as we hear, so we respond: adoration and praise in the face of who he is; thanksgiving and love in the face of whom he made us; repentance and reparation in the face of whom we have made ourselves.

At times our experience of him, of the reality of what is, of who he is, who we are, our relation, is so full that no words, thoughts, feelings or images are adequate. The only fitting response is that of our whole being. In silence, we are to him—communion—*contemplatio*. "Be still, and know that I am God."

This is the basic fabric of all Christian prayer, God has spoken—the eternal Word made incarnate—and we respond. No matter how simple or how complex our way may be, no matter how sophisticated the method we employ, our prayer is essentially this. All methods, all ritual, all symbols, have their purpose in letting God's word to us evoke from us a total response.

Father Tom Kane, with a rich simplicity and directness, invites us to experience this. His very open sharing, as a man of faith and gentle love, invites us to take courage and hope to pursue a richer and fuller prayer life. Father wrote these pages as a very busy man, teaching several college courses, providing guidance to innumerable students, serving a busy parish. In the face of such witness, our pleas of being too busy to make time to sit down and listen to the Lord come across as quite hollow. We find the time to do the things we deem important: eat, sleep, share with loved ones, even watch TV. Who loves us more and is more to be loved than the Lord? What is more important—the physical life sustained by food and rest, or the eternal life of our spirit that needs to be nourished and rested in prayer?

Father writes in the spirit of the ancient Christian tradition, but he writes as a man of *today*. He makes the fruit of the Christian heritage readily available. He writes for the students he teaches and guides—quite ordinary, confused and searching American teenagers. He writes for the people he serves in the parish—mothers and fathers, grandparents and singles, those who come each Sunday to celebrate Mass with him and listen to his homilies, who catch him in the sacristy or come to the rectory to pour out their troubles, share their joys, seek advice. Father shares here his own way of prayer, his own life in the Lord, which has made him a most loving and loved spiritual father and friend. We are grateful to him.

M. Basil Pennington, O.C.S.O.

Preface

How did these pages get written? The fact is that they came out of my own attempts to pray. After praying over a gospel story in the way I describe in the first chapter, I would try to catch in words something of what had happened in me. Gradually I found that the more I could do this the more others seemed to identify with it. Where I was most myself I seemed to be most like others; and my struggles with prayer and words seemed to help them. That led to a series of talks, then some articles in *Desert Call*, and finally this litle book.

When I set about doing the book I first wrote the introductory chapter to show how I tried to pray. Then there was a chapter to say something of how I looked at Jesus. Following that I selected some of the images that dominate the Gospels. As I lived through and wrote the different chapters, I came to see that what happened to me as I moved from image to image followed very closely the teachings of John of the Cross. So I tried to refer to him in the footnotes, hoping that this, too, might help some people. At the end I threw in a post-script to connect what I had written with some questions that I thought might be in some peoples' minds.

Now, it is my happy task to thank, publicly, four friends who helped me in this, as they have helped me in my attempts to live it: Sr. Nadine McGuinness who first got me thinking about it; Sr. Frances McHugh of St. Francis' College, Letchworth, where parts of this were written; Thomas Halloran whose words and wisdom are sprinkled about these pages; and Sr. Miriam Cecile Lenehan whose least gift to me was her patience in typing the manuscript.

Journey of the Heart

Introduction—Metaphors for Faith

This little book is not about prayer. It is, rather, an invitation into a way of prayer. It's not the only way. I would never claim that it is the best way. But it is a way I have found helpful and I invite you into it. Let us begin by looking at Luke 11:1-4.

> He was praying in a certain place, and when he ceased, one of his disciples said to him, "Lord, teach us to pray, as John taught his disciples." And he said to them, "When you pray, say:
> 'Father, hallowed be thy name. Thy kingdom come. Give us each day our daily bread; and forgive us our sins, for we ourselves forgive everyone who is indebted to us; and lead us not into temptation.'"

After being with Jesus, after seeing him pray, the disciples gradually come to see that really they do not know how to pray. And so they go to him, the one who knows how to pray; and he teaches them. I think this was true of the first disciples and that it remains true for all of us who have followed in their place. We really don't know how to pray; and yet somehow we, like Peter and John, know we have to pray. So we, too, must go to Jesus and let him teach us. As I think back on my own life I can see that first he taught me through my parents. My mother knelt down beside my bed with me when I was a little boy and taught me the words of the "Our Father." She taught me Jesus' prayer. I'm sure that once I had gotten all the words down I assumed I could now pray "like all the big people." But her teaching didn't just reach to the words. Really she taught me more by the way she said them. The trust and simplicity I experienced beside me taught me more than the words. From her I learned that I had to give my very heart. In a sense, two things were going on. I was being invited into a form of prayer, the words; but on a deeper level I was also being drawn into the very heart of prayer: surrender to God. This deeper rhythm is at the heart of all prayer. It is the moment of transforming grace. That moment when our hearts catch fire and we know that our true destiny is to give them away to the Beloved who calls us.

This twofold dimension to prayer seems to be a constant. There is the form, the words, the place, the whole symbolic and ritual context. There is also the deeper rhythm; there is surrender to God. As a disciple I must go back again and again to the form, to the rosary, the eucharist, or some kind of meditation, for there Jesus is gradually teaching me to pray. He is opening up my heart and yours to that deeper rhythm of his own life, surrender to the Father. He is teaching us to pray the "Our Father." This little book, then, will invite you into one of these ways of prayer, one of those places where the Lord might teach you to pray.

This entering into the deeper rhythm of prayer can be understood as a deepening ability to listen. When people talk to others they have a tendency to listen almost exclusively to themselves. Their own feelings and needs are so intense, so demanding that they can hear little else. So they engage in conversation, but when they are not speaking they aren't really listening, for they are thinking about what they will say next. Or they are listening for what they want to hear, not what the other person might be trying to say. But something else can happen, as with real friends or loved ones. Here the love we have for our friends can lead us on to discipline ourselves so that we are very careful to listen to what they say. Years of such careful and loving listening can deepen this so that we come to listen in a new way. We don't just listen to the words, though we find we are doing that better and better. Rather, we listen right through the words to the people themselves. We come to discover that we are constantly listening to discern what is going on in them. So you have: hearing mostly one's self, listening *to* what another says and listening *through* what another says to who they are.

This seems to be very similar to what happens to us when we pray. At first we listen, but mostly we hear ourselves. We hear our fears, our loneliness, our need to be loved and loving. And out of that we listen to hear how God will help us. This is very much like the little boy who accidently breaks a window and at night prays that God, "who always hears our prayers," will make everything all right by the morning. Now there can be a real element of faith here, one that is quite appropriate for a boy of 6 or 7. But this is not as appropriate at 17 and even less so at 37. Just as we can grow to the point where we can really listen to the words of those we love, so we can come to listen to the words of Jesus in a deeper way. This is what meditation is all about. The point is to listen to the words of Jesus as if my whole life depended on it—and indeed it does! It is to listen to God in utter simplicity without defending myself against him in any way.

To listen like this, I find I have to be more than silent. I have to wait until I become still, until I become totally quiet. That stillness, in faith, in hope, is the very stillness of God. This is what it means, I think, to put one's self in the very presence of God. At the same time each day I go to my quiet place. I know a woman who does this in her car after she has done the day's shopping and a man who does it as he commutes to work on the train. Wherever it is, I sit down and try to open my heart to the mystery of God's presence. Gradually I become still. But it seems that I do not create the stillness. I empty myself of noisy chatter. I lay down the preoccupations of the day, and the stillness comes upon me.

In that stillness, I read the gospel stories, but this is not at all like my usual reading. I do not attack the text with my mind. I listen. Deeply I listen. That listening comes out of direct and simple faith. "What is *he* saying to me now?" Slowly I turn the words over, holding them in my heart. I go back to them again and again. Sometimes I try to climb into the stories by using my imagination. I picture the whole scene so that I can better hear what the story is really saying. Sometimes this prayerful, simple reading catches me so deeply that I cannot go on. I stop and the imagining that accompanies the reading seems to pause and I am just *there*. I am held *there*, but I cannot say where or by whom, though I hope and trust it is God, even in God. Much more passively, yet much more attuned, more peacefully receptive, I wait. When I wander off, I read again. Gradually the spaces widen out. I drift off less and less; and the stillness, the waiting, the listening is deeper. I am beginning to listen right through the words. Because of that I am not quick to search for a word to express what is being spoken to me. Sometimes ideas are crucial; but mostly he speaks to me in a way deeper than words. I sit there listening and listening. Sometimes I read; more and more I wait. More and more the waiting, the listening is given to me. Always I try to keep still.

This listening to the words of Jesus, this prayerful but disciplined entrance into the gospel stories begins to change our lives. It is as if it were a mirror held up to my life and I can discern there what is happening and not happening in my life. Now, there are two poles to this. There is a coming to know one's self. But there is also a coming to know Jesus as he is presented in the gospels. As we move into these stories and we hear what they are really saying we are confronted by the Lord and what he has to say about us and our lives. For if we are really faithful to the gospel stories, if we don't impose our meanings on them, but slowly learn to let them disclose their meaning to us and in that illumine and transform our lives, then the Lord of the gospels will have become the Lord of our lives.

This ability to transform human living is written into the stories of the gospels and the structures of our lives. The facts of most peoples' lives are often similar, more so than we usually notice. For all of us there is birth and death, loneliness and tragedy. There is waiting, remorse, disappointment, confusion; and sometimes there are moments of illumination when we know it is all worthwhile. There is work and hope and quite often fidelity. Those who learn to live their lives within these stories of the gospels seem to be gifted with an ability to see a huge meaning in these facts of human living. For them marriage is not just living together; it is a sacrament. Death is not the final calamitous end; it is a kind of birth. Waiting is not just passing time, for it can be transformed into a way of sharing in the way God holds us gently in his hand. This is to transform the often confusing and painful facts of our lives into mysteries by discovering the deep meaning that under-lies them, but which we usually tend to miss.

To do this we need images, symbols, metaphors, stories that disclose this deep meaning, that help us glimpse it, and so let it surface in and transform our lives. This is what the gospel stories do. The evangelists collected and developed

stories and images that carried and unleashed the startlingly
new way Jesus had of living and dying. These stories and
metaphors were handed on and accepted in faith in such a
way that there was a transformation of the images by which
and within which people lived. Further, this is something
many people have experienced. For example, recall, for a
moment, one of the times when a gospel story really came
alive for you, when all of a sudden you knew it from the
inside, when you could discover yourself in the story, where
you *were* Peter or the woman taken in adultery. Wasn't it
because you had really connected with the basic symbols of
the story; and they had let you see, in a new way, who the
Lord was calling you to be? Still, we must be careful here.
This must not be an attempt to make up images that appeal
to us, but to hand ourselves over to the images that come
from Jesus and are presented to us in the gospel tradition:
the grain of wheat, the lavishly generous father, Jesus'
choice of powerlessness before Pilate.

We have been talking about transforming the facts of our
lives into mysteries. When you do that, you both disclose a
deeper dimension of reality at the same time that you open
yourself up to that reality. The two always go together. It is
only as I change that I can see what was always there, but
never recognized and so what was lost on me. But I change
by living in the image, the metaphor, the parable. It is
precisely the image that gradually frees my imagination so
that I can see and live what I never noticed before. We will,
then, be involved in a study of Christology when we try to
discover some of the underlying images and metaphors of
the Jesus tradition. When we push on and try to see how
those images echo in our lives we will be involved in an
exercise in Christian self-discovery.

To pray over the gospel stories in the way I have been

trying to describe changes us. But I have found that if I stay with the same story the confrontation gradually becomes deeper. I'll go back to the same story every day for a week or ten days. Gradually it seems to sink deeply into my heart. When I get up in the morning, it is with me. If I'm taking a walk or driving somewhere, it will come upon me. It is, kind of, all around me, present to me, helping me see myself in terms of the story, or even in the story. The images flood over me, overwhelm me; and right there I discover who I am, who the Lord is making me.

Or, I'll spend a whole day, my day in the desert, going back to a story again and again. I'll pray over it for an hour then go for a walk and then come back to it again. After mass I'll try to submerge myself in it again, slowly letting the images seep into me. I'll do this four or five times. As this happens the story comes alive in me. I don't just understand Zacchaeus (Lk. 19:1-10); I become him. I have his fears, his illusions. "I'm desperate, but he can't be interested in me. I'm a sinner." And then Jesus calls out, "It really is you I want," and then I'm not just dealing with ideas. I'm confronted by the Lord. I can hear the unexpected, the unheard of, that he wants me. My world crumbles. Right here, in this revelation of the Lord's love for me, I am freed from some of my illusions. Or I can listen to the same story from the vantage point of those who think they are so good and are so hard that they can't rejoice that a man has been touched by God. My self-righteous world crumbles, and I sit there stunned.

Let me try to illustrate this. Luke 5:1-11 can serve as example.

> While the people pressed upon him to hear the word of God, he was standing by the lake of Gennesaret. And he saw two boats by the lake; but the fishermen had gone out of them and

were washing their nets. Getting into one of the boats, which was Simon's, he asked him to put out a little from the land. And he sat down and taught the people from the boat. And when he had ceased speaking, he said to Simon, "Put out into the deep and let down your nets for a catch." And Simon answered, "Master, we toiled all night and took nothing! But at your word I will let down the nets." And when they had done this, they enclosed a great shoal of fish; and as their nets were breaking, they beckoned to their partners in the other boat to come and help them. And they came and filled both boats, so that they began to sink. But when Simon Peter saw it, he fell down at Jesus' knees, saying, "Depart from me, for I am a sinful man, O Lord." For he was astonished, and all that were with him, at the catch of fish which they had taken; and so also were James and John, sons of Zebedee, who were partners with Simon. And Jesus said to Simon, "Do not be afraid; henceforth you will be catching men." And when they had brought their boats to land, they left everything and followed him.

To enter into this, imagine something you have done of which you are profoundly ashamed, something that reminds you of your ingrained selfishness. Now, holding that in your memory and painfully aware of it, imagine yourself in the presence of Jesus. It becomes very awkward, doesn't it? Could not Peter's words become your own? "Depart from me, for I am a sinful man, O Lord." If you can understand this; more, if you can enter into and live it, you can enter into and live half of the story. But to stop here, to think this is what the story means is to radically misunderstand the story. It is not to be imaginative enough. It is not to have a Christian imagination, because in the story Jesus sees things in a radically different way than does Peter.

Jesus sees the waywardness, the fear, the illusions, that characterize Peter and his whole way of living. Actually he sees them much more clearly than does Peter. But he also loves Peter and sees what he could be, what he needs to be; and he calls him to that. He asks Peter to follow him, to trust in his vision, and in that to be healed and transformed, so that he can be sent to heal others in Jesus' name. Gradually it happens. Now, to be a believer is not just to accept the credal statements about Jesus, though they have their place. Nor is it to be able to understand what Peter feels in this story. It is to feel what Peter feels and then to realize that there is more to it than that. It is to recognize that Jesus' view of Peter is the only truly real one. Furthermore, it is to turn this story over and over again in one's heart until one knows Peter from the inside, until one hears Jesus' saving, healing, word that is addressed to Peter, addressed to one's very self and to accept it, trust in it and live on it. Then the word of God ceases to be a word unheard and explodes in its transformative power into my life and yours.

Baptism and Desert

Where should one start to listen to Jesus? In a sense it doesn't matter so long as one starts. But the beatitudes are as good a place as any.

As I sit down in the presence of the Lord and open my heart to him I hear:

Blessed are the poor in spirit, for theirs is the kingdom of heaven.

Blessed are the meek, for they shall inherit the earth.

Blessed are those who hunger and thirst for righteousness, for they shall be satisfied.

Blessed are the merciful, for they shall obtain mercy.

Blessed are the pure in heart, for they shall see God.

Blessed are the peacemakers, for they shall be called sons of God.

Blessed are those who are persecuted for righteousness' sake, for theirs is the kingdom of heaven.

Blessed are you when men revile you and persecute you and utter all kinds of evil against you falsely on my account. Rejoice and be glad, for your reward is great in heaven, for so men persecuted the prophets who were before you.
(Matthew 5:3-12)

Turning these words of the Lord over in my heart, taking them seriously, I begin to realize that even as I try to hear what the Lord is saying, I listen as an outsider. I don't usually think of the poor, the meek, the lowly, those who hunger for righteousness, the persecuted as blessed, as overcome with good fortune. With most people I tend to think that to be rich, to have a good time, to be powerful and free of pain and persecution is to be happy. As I let these words echo within me I sense what a stranger I am to Jesus and have to admit that his vision scares me. It might cost too much. Yet even in the midst of this fear something draws me. This vision frightens me, to live in it would turn my world inside out and upside down, but it also catches my heart and I somehow know that my heart will always be restless until I live in the beatitudes. As this seeps into me I begin to wonder: what was Jesus like that he could say such things. What was his sense of reality, for that was what lay behind the beatitudes and all of his words and actions that so scandalized many of the people who met him? If I could discover that, even more, if I could enter into that viewpoint, the viewpoint of Jesus, then the beatitudes and the parables and the disturbing actions of Jesus might turn out to make great sense, and my heart might be at peace.

The gospels seem to point to Jesus' baptism. Something seems to have happened there that changed his life. He never again went back to his former life as the carpenter at Nazareth. Further, Mark 11:28-33 also seems to bring us back to the baptism. When Jesus is asked, "By what authority are you doing these things?" the immediate reference is the cleansing of the temple, but in a sense it also refers back to all the things he has done and said. And his counter-question, whether the baptism of John was from God or not, is not an evasion. He is implying that his authority rests on what happened to him when he was baptized in the Jordan.

In those days Jesus came from Nazareth of Galilee and was baptized by John in the Jordan. And when he came up out of the water, immediately he saw the heavens opened and the

Spirit descending upon him like a dove; and a voice came from heaven, "Thou art my beloved Son; with thee I am well pleased" (Mark 1:9-11).

As you pray this over again and again, what dawns in your heart is that at his baptism Jesus had an overwhelming experience of being accepted by God his Father. In a completely unearned, and seemingly unexpected way the spirit of God filled Jesus. Who was Jesus? He was the Beloved of his Father. As these words sink into my heart I start to marvel at the gift that this was. Jesus did not have to earn this; he could not lose it. The Father just loved him; and that love was unconditional. This is so different from what we usually meet. "I'll love you if . . ." or "I'll love you because . . ." Here it is simply, "You are my Beloved." That's who Jesus was; and as I hear this I also begin to recognize that that's who I need to be. I can only be my true self when I am Jesus, when I am the beloved of the Father. In a way I had never guessed, but in a way that has always haunted me, Jesus is who I desperately need to be. This comes crashing in on me as I go back to the text and let it wash over me.

Beyond anything Jesus had to earn or merit, the Father has graciously revealed himself to his Son; and there are absolutely no conditions on this gift of the Father's acceptance and love. Because of the Father's unbounded goodness, he loves his son and at the baptism this seems to have dawned on Jesus in a new way. This seems to open up to us the deep significance of Jesus' calling God *Abba*. The word has a long history,[1] but at the time of Jesus it was used by little children in addressing their fathers. The English "daddy" comes close to meaning the same thing. Even adults came to use it of their beloved and respected fathers. But this most intimate form of address was not used by Palestinian Jews as a form of address to God. It would have sounded disrespectful, even presumptuous to Jesus' contemporaries. Indeed, "*we do not have a single example* of God being addressed as *abba* in Judaism, but Jesus *always* addressed God in this way in his prayers."[2] The uniqueness of Jesus' way of addressing God brings us to the very heart of his religious experience and vision. He could approach his Father with a sense of absolute and unquestionable trust and intimacy. He spoke to the Father with the simplicity and directness of a little child, freely accepting his dependence on the Father, in the full assurance of his unconditional love. Indeed, we see him exulting in this.

> I thank thee, Father, Lord of heaven and earth, that thou hast hidden these things from the wise and understanding and revealed them to babes; yea, Father, for such was thy gracious will. All things have been delivered to me by my Father; and no one knows the Father except the Son and anyone to whom the Son chooses to reveal him (Matthew 11:25-27).

This clearly brings out the personal aspect of Jesus' intimacy with the Father. It also starts to speak of his mission, which flowed out of his union with the Father.

From the time of his baptism Jesus seems to have been conscious that he was authorized to proclaim the good news of the Father's unbounded love. What had happened in him was the true destiny of all reality. Everyone, all of creation, had to know the Father's love and come alive in it. This Kingdom of God, where the loving concern of the Father would break forth, was at hand. It was just around the corner. In fact, it had already begun in Jesus. But how was he to respond to the gift of the Father and share this with others?

> The spirit immediately drove him out into the wilderness. And he was in the wilderness forty days, tempted by Satan; and he was with the wild beasts; and the angels ministered to him. (Mark 1:12)

The Spirit that anoints Jesus at the baptism, that over-whelms him with his Father's love, immediately drives him out into the wilderness of temptation and decision. How should he respond? There was no going back to Nazareth as a carpenter; but where should he go? If unconditional acceptance was the gift of the Father, purity of heart was Jesus' response. Jesus was pure of heart in the sense that he was totally simple. He found his sense of security, his identity, his reality in his Father's love and in nothing else. He did not, then, have to try to live off power, or wealth, or comfort, or prestige, or pleasure, or his good name. The love of the Father alone sufficed. The love of the Father was enough, gracious and life giving beyond measure. The desert makes clear that if you try to seek security in anything other than the Father's love you are ultimately trapped in idolatry. You *believe* in that thing. You expect, you hope, that it will make you real. Jesus did not do that. He loved the Father with all his heart, all his soul, all his mind. He took the first commandment literally. He seems to have believed in the love of his Father so much that he didn't have to look for something else to keep him going.

This trust in the Father alone determined how he would proclaim the good news of the Father's Kingdom. In the way he lived and in his preaching, Jesus invited men to prepare for the Kingdom: to repent, to trust in his Father and in that get a first glimpse of what was coming. But he did that in purity of heart.

As things worked out that entailed his leaving behind home, family, comfort, reputation, physical integrity and safety as he took the place of the now imprisoned man who had called him to his baptism (Mk. 1:14-15). At the heart of this was his choice to rely on his Father and not at all on his own power or influence. This is the point of the temptations in Luke 4:1-13 and the reason for the stern rebuke to Peter and the other disciples in Mark 8:30-33. Before he left the desert Jesus chose to proclaim the Kingdom in purity of heart. You can see this in the way he treats everyone he meets. The Kingdom was the Father's gift and Jesus seems to have handed over both the fruit of his mission and the means he would use in it to his Father as he wrestled in the desert. It would be the Father's work from beginning to end, caused by the miracle of his love, and by nothing else.

It is one thing to do this before embarking on such a mission, when one can hope and pray that this ultimate simplicity will bear fruit. It is something else again to still be trusting as that mission collapses about you. This leads us to a contrast that is implicit in the gospel stories, but which brings to light a crucial ingredient: the deepening character of purity of heart. The contrast is between Judas and Jesus. As you read over the gospels it begins to be clear that as Jesus' mission collapsed, Judas and Jesus had to deal with fundamental decisions. The story that both had been living, each in his own way, of setting out with God to bring the Kingdom, becomes a story of surrender to the mysterious Kingdom God is creating beyond anything man can understand or experience. At this point Judas cracks. He cannot trust that much. On the other hand Jesus says, "Yes, even here: especially here." That surrender was interpreted in the symbols Jesus had at hand. As everything collapsed around him, Jesus took the great symbols of his tradition and interpreted his life in terms of them. There was a new exodus taking place in his passage; and his blood would somehow be the blood of a new convenant (Mk. 14: 22-25). This interpretation seems to have allowed Jesus to glimpse the deep mystery of the Father's love that was working itself out in the harsh facts of his life. Purity of heart grew deeper.

In the last crisis of his life, Jesus is engulfed in darkness. He prays; but now it is very dark. The darkness of sin and terror the massive evil that grips the world, crowds in on him. Jesus prays in the darkness of the Mount of Olives and the Father seems so silent. Beyond what he can understand, beyond the support his followers give him, Jesus chooses to trust in his Father. The Father is gracious beyond measure even in the darkness of the garden. This trust is most stark on the cross. Abandoned by all, when the whole thing is in shambles, and when the Father does not seem close, Jesus still, with rock-like fidelity, proclaims the Father's gracious reign. In his death agony he begins that great prayer of faith rising out of the very verge of despair. He prays Psalm 22: "My God, My God, why have you forsaken me?"

Purity of heart is pushed to the extreme. In his passion and death Jesus had to choose his Father at a much more radical level than he could ever have done before. He had to reach out to the Father in purity of heart as everything else went. This is crucial. When Jesus gave up control of his actions, when he handed over the fruits of his work as a preacher to the Father, that entailed purity of heart. It was an expression of it. Purity of heart could be seen as operative in his life. But when he dies on the cross, it is not just another expression of purity of heart. The very ultimacy of that action makes manifest that purity of heart was the whole meaning of his life. When Jesus chose the Father from the cross he reached out to him as everything else went, even the experience of the Father. There was no psychic resource, no facet of his spirit, no fiber of his body that was not involved in that choice: God alone. In a very real sense Jesus became his act of trust in the Father.

In his symbolic actions and in his words Jesus was constantly inviting others to come over and share in his relationship to his Father. The twelfth chapter of Luke is just one example of this. Jesus is talking about fear.

> Do not fear those who kill the body, and after that have no more they can do (v. 4)
> Do not be anxious about your life, what you shall eat, nor about your body, what you shall put on (v. 22)
> Fear not little flock, for it is your Father's good pleasure to give you the kingdom. Sell your possessions and give alms . . . (v. 32-33)

It seems that most people really don't believe what Jesus is saying here. Indeed, as I take these words into my heart I find I scarcely believe them, for I am afraid. I find it so hard to believe what Jesus himself believed, what was revealed to him at his baptism, namely that the Father really does love us with an unconditioned love. Because so many of us don't live with a deep sense of this, we must seek our security somewhere else. Most people seem to live with the lurking fear that the universe doesn't care about them, and that one day it will collapse on them and snuff them out without ever noticing or caring. Further, the life experiences of many people only reinforce this brooding sense of vulnerability. This is the primordial terror. To live with it, and with our concomitantly diminished sense of ourselves, we move out to things and to other people, to do exactly what Jesus is warning us against in this passage. We worry about a whole raft of things, for our insecurity, our fear and our alienation bind us into a rapacious possessiveness as we desperately attempt to cover over our terror.

Out of my desperation comes a series of false hopes. If I am beautiful, if I can be witty, then they will notice me. At least part of the universe will pay attention to me. I will not be so alone.

If I can surround myself with comfort, with security, I will hide in it. At least for a while I will feel safe.

If I drench myself with pleasure, either booze, or drugs, or sex, or whatever, then for a while I will make this frightening universe serve me, care about me. I can lose my terrified self in that pleasure.

The litany could go on and on; and it would have to deal with money, power, control. But the point is always the same. Deeply anxious, aware that I am not all that I need to be, and terrified by an uncaring universe, I go out to manipulate what I can of that universe. I try to make it serve me, pay attention to me. I try to twist, control, manipulate. But it doesn't work. It does not bring real peace, for it is only a momentary escape; and I know it. Slowly I learn that even this fleeting promise is a delusion. The lurking terror remains: it will collapse on me as I fear.

But, if a man could believe that the universe was on his side, if he could really experience what Jesus is talking about in the gospel stories—that there is nothing to fear because his Father loves us—would that not transform his life? I think it would. Such a man would still go out to people and to things, but now the motive would be changed. It would no longer be desperation that would drive him but compassion. If a man really came to believe this, he would have to let everyone know what he now knew: we are not alone for the Father loves us. Such a transformation of terror into compassion would free a man to love his world and the people in it in a startlingly new way. Indeed, if I could believe what Jesus says to me here in Luke's gospel that I, too, am the Father's beloved, my life would come to resemble the transformed life I see him living on the pages of the gospels.

This invitation comes through in story after story.

He sat down opposite the treasury, and watched the multitude putting money into the treasury. Many rich people put in large

sums. And a poor widow came, and put in two copper coins,
which make a penny. And he called his disciples to him, and
said to them, "Truly, I say to you, this poor widow has put in
more than all those who are contributing to the treasury. For
they all contributed out of their abundance; but she out of her
poverty has put in everything she had, her whole living."
(Mark 12:41-44)

As we listen to this simple story the great faith of the woman
confronts us. As Mark carefully presents this story, he
emphasizes that she is a poor widow, someone for whom all
the normal human supports are lacking or have been taken
away. Then she gives both coins. She could have given one,
kept the other for herself, and still have been enormously
generous. But she gives away all, committing herself completely to God's mercy. As we listen the invitation to live with
the same simplicity haunts us.

You can see this in reverse in Mark 10:17-28. The rich
young man is quite good, but his heart is divided. His needs
bind him to his riches. Without them life is not just difficult,
it is unimaginable. When Jesus invites him to give away his
wealth and learn to trust only in the Father, this turns out to
be the one thing he cannot do. That provokes a discussion
between Jesus and his disciples, during which two very
different senses of reality are manifested. Because Jesus is
liberated by his knowledge of the Father's love, he does not
need to seek his security in wealth or power. But this is not
yet true for the rich young man or for the disciples. They
cannot see what Jesus sees, that these are only phantoms
which promise safety, reality, depth of life to those who are
trapped in their own needs. They cannot deliver. There is
really nothing there. They cannot give life. Ultimately there
is only the Father's love. At the end of the dialogue, Jesus
concludes by saying that only a miracle of God's love can
free a man to see this. A miracle like his own baptism? In

any case, the parables, and the eating with sinners, his unconventional behavior, all seem to be occasions for this miracle. They challenge and reverse the human way of looking at reality and open up a frightening but incredibly rich world of graciousness. It is frightening because if I really listen to Jesus my human and egocentric world collapses. It is gracious because that opens up to me the world God creates. With the startling strangeness of these words and deeds, the idols I have made for myself and my selfish needs begin to crack and collapse. The word, which is really the Word of God, breaks through on me to rearrange my whole way of life. In a flash, in that crumbling of a whole way of viewing reality, the Word of God ceases to be a word unheard.

This word that echoes within me is Jesus' word inviting me to enter into and share in his stance toward reality. It is this stance that lies behind the beatitudes. One's stance toward reality seems to be determined by what one cares about. The love Jesus experienced as coming to him as an unconditional gift from his Father enabled him to care about all reality. He wanted the rest of reality to know what he knew: that there was nothing to fear. To come, then, to care about all of reality, to become universally compassionate, to be able to mourn with those in sorrow; to be meek with all; to hunger and thirst that all might know the saving righteousness of the Father; to be a peacemaker; would that not mean that one had passed over into the very stance of Jesus? And to be free enough to do that, wouldn't one have to be as free as Jesus was? And would not the source of that liberation have to be the same love of the Father?

Surely living in this way might entail persecution and suffering, as it did with Jesus. Again a passing over. "Blessed are those who are persecuted for righteousness' sake." But might not the liberating love of the Father, that was at the very heart of such a stance, fill a man or woman with a deep sense of peace, a peace so deep that no suffering or persecution could take it away? Perhaps then the words of Jesus, "I come to give you peace, a peace that the world cannot give," would take on a new meaning, and be heard as if for the first time. Such a man would be free enough to accept Jesus' invitation to travel with him as he moves through the world and across our lives. He could worry about all reality, feel its pains and compassionately understand its terrors and at the same time be grasped by ultimate serenity because he knew that ultimately there was nothing to fear.

That leaves two beatitudes untouched. "Blessed are the pure in heart, for they shall see God." To be pure in heart means to love one thing. It means that a man or woman is so simple, so free, that they can find all their security in God alone. This is the only adequate response to the Father's unconditional love. To seek your security in another person or thing is to be idolatrous. Even to hedge your bet is to fall into this. The first beatitude that deals with property refers to this, for possessions or any kind of riches can be a danger to purity of heart. This was the case with the rich young man of Mark 10:17-23. Therefore, the man whose life is not cluttered up with many things, who can love with compassion, is free to be pure of heart. As the beatitudes promise, when a man is totally simple, when everything else he could cling to is gone, either given up or burnt away, then he can see God.

---

[1]For background on this see Joachim Jeremias, *New Testament Theology*. N.Y.: Scribners, 1971, pp.61-68.

[2]*Ibid.*, p. 66, italics his.

Call and Journey

Towards the end of the previous chapter I suggested that the gift of God's love frees us to accept Jesus' invitation to travel with him as he moves through the world and across our lives. Mark 1:16-20 can bring this home to us.

> And passing by the Sea of Galilee, he saw Simon and Andrew the brother of Simon casting a net into the sea; for they were fishermen. And Jesus said to them, "Follow me and I will make you become fishers of men." And immediately they left their nets and followed him. And going on a little farther, he saw James the son of Zebedee and John his brother, who were in their boat mending the nets. And immediately he called them; and they left their father Zebedee in the boat with the hired servants, and followed him.

As you turn this over in your heart it is at first very familiar. But as this listening deepens it can begin to jar us. The call of Jesus comes out of the blue. As it is presented here in Mark, this is the first meeting between Jesus and his future disciples. He comes up to them, calls them and immediately, without a word of explanation, they walk away from their old lives and follow him. Once this dawns on us the familiar story that had always made sense no longer does. That drives us back to the context that Mark has prepared in the first fifteen verses, because the story makes sense only in that context.

We are dealing here with the unspeakable, literally unimaginable, hope that comes upon us from beyond and that is the fruit of God's healing and creative love. For that reason theologians would name it an eschatological call. It is a glimpse of a way of life that is not scarred by the betrayal that mars even our most faithful living. It is a vision of a universe that makes sense, where slavery to sin is broken, where death is transformed into life, where loneliness, terror and guilt are healed. Exactly what such deep life, such a healed universe would look like, we do not know. We cannot say, though we hint at it in images: "heaven," "the banquet," "the wedding feast." But in those images, sometimes, we can glimpse it. And the glimpse of it, the living hope for it, heals our minds and begins to free our hearts for their true destiny. In the depths of our hearts we are moved in a way we cannot explain, but we know without doubt that it was for this that we were made. In our story Jesus as the Baptized One, and this is what Mark has set up in the opening verses of the gospel, as he who has been anointed in the Spirit of God, is sent to proclaim this great hope. So it is that when he speaks he cuts right through the disciples' hearts. Peter and Andrew, James and John, can't tell you exactly what has happened. But what their hearts have always longed for, what they have often looked for in the wrong place, opens before them in a flash. They follow him. And because their hearts are so full, they walk away from things that up until then had seemed so important.

As you and I listen to this story from Peter and Andrew's viewpoint, as that prayerful listening gradually seeps into us enabling us to grow into the story, it can remind us of all those times in the past when God's love touched us and filled us with an unspeakable hope. It brings back that moment when we first felt called to religious life, or when marriage started to reveal its hidden mystery. Or we recall the baptism of a child when we were filled with wild, unutterable hopes for one we loved so much; or silent moments in prayer when our heart sang, moved by a melody of eternal stillness. Indeed, as you pray over this story now, turning it over in your heart again and again, it happens within you. You are Peter. You can hear his call, "Follow me." Right now you are the one who is being called. Beyond anything I can understand this experience breaks upon me calling me to believe that we are called to a destiny beyond our comprehension. A beloved calls me to an intimacy, a depth, a surrender, a fruition that is beyond words, but the only true homeland of my heart.

To go with him the disciples had to leave much behind, much that was good. But in terms of this great call, all will be transformed. Still, in a real sense what they most truly are will remain, for they will stay fishermen. But now they will be fishers for this mysterious Kingdom that they have glimpsed for a moment. What that will look like, or what it will cost, they do not know. Jesus will do it. "And I will make you become fishers of men." They follow him. That same call echoes now in my heart and yours, calling us to follow this mysterious One who captivates our hearts, to leave behind old ways. This is the beginning of a journey.

Matthew 14:22-33 might help us to see something of what it might look like at certain moments in the midst of this journey.

> Then he made the disciples get into the boat and go before him to the other side, while he dismissed the crowds. And after he had dismissed the crowds, he went up on the mountain by himself to pray. When evening came, he was there alone, but the boat by this time was many furlongs distant from the land, beaten by the waves; for the wind was against them. And in the fourth watch of the night he came to them, walking on the sea. But when the disciples saw him walking on the sea, they were terrified, saying, "It is a ghost!" And they cried out for fear. But immediately he spoke to them saying, "Take heart, it is I; have no fear."

And Peter answered him, "Lord, if it is you, bid me come to you on the water." He said, "Come." So Peter got out of the boat and walked on the water and came to Jesus; but when he saw the wind, he was afraid, and beginning to sink he cried out, "Lord, save me." Jesus immediately reached out his hand and caught him, saying to him, "O man of little faith, why did you doubt?" And when they got into the boat, the wind ceased. And those in the boat worshipped him saying, "Truly you are the Son of God."

Once again we can listen to this from Peter's viewpoint. Peter has followed Jesus. He has listened to him and lived with him. That has brought him to the point here, where Jesus sends him out onto the sea that quickly becomes a chaos. Jesus is no longer there, and the universe howls about him. As you and I gradually move into the story this begins to remind us so much of our own lives. We, too, have tried to listen to Jesus, to follow him, to journey through life with him. Charged with his vision he has sent us out on our mission in life and we have gone out with high hopes. Then he doesn't seem to be there. Maybe it is our own life or the lives of loved ones that seem to be swamped by the frenzy. And we are so afraid. The vision of peace and integrity, of lives healed by the presence of the Lord crumbles before us. We are stunned, terrified as everything of any value seems to collapse around us and we don't know what to do.

Then we have pictured for us not just the man from Nazareth but the Anointed of the Father, the bringer of God's peace and order, striding across the seas of chaos and through our lives telling us: "Take heart, it is I; have no fear." In the very midst of the chaos he calls on us to believe that he has conquered the confusion, the awful mindless violence that crushes our world and our hearts. Here Peter has to wonder if it is a ghost, and so do we. Is this all a dream? Is my whole life of faith nothing but an illusion? Is it only because I am too timid to face the real terrors of life, that I find myself hiding in these consoling pipe dreams of this Jesus? Then the call, the call reminiscent of that call that first stirred our hearts, is heard: "Come." Stirred to faith we leave behind the boat that protects us from the pain and confusion that whirls about us, and trusting in the One who calls us we walk safely amid the chaos.

Peter takes his eyes off Jesus; he concentrates on the strength of the wind and filled with fear he begins to sink. This, too, is so very much like us. As we sit quietly, turning the story over in our hearts, the fears that fill our lives, the places where the ingested chaos lurks, start to come to the surface. The fear of being unacceptable, of really having to take responsibility for our own lives, the unspeakable fears of failure and death surge within us. We remember how we have gone with Jesus in the past only to panic when these terrors caught us off guard. Indeed, as we live in the heart of this story we can once again feel ourselves begin to sink; but guided by the story we cry out, "Lord, save me." And he is right there with us in the midst of the story catching hold of us as we journey with him. With that some of the fear is broken; trust has entered a little deeper into us.

This theme of journeying with Jesus is central to Mark's gospel.[1] It is there in the very way he structures it. In the first half of the gospel Jesus invites men to believe in him and in that begin to experience the Kingdom of his Father. Very often this only leads to rejection. In 3:1-6 it is the leaders of the people. In 6:1-6 it is his own townsfolk. From Peter's profession of faith in 8:27-30, Jesus turns his face towards Jerusalem and his final destiny. With chapter 11 he enters Jerusalem. This great journey of the disciples with Jesus,

---

[1]For more on this see E. Schweizer, *The Good News According to Mark.* Richmond, Va.: John Knox Press, 1970.

then, covers chapters 8 to 11; and as you read it there is an increasing awareness that this is parallel to our lives as believers. We, too, are on a journey with Jesus; and the individual stories have a peculiar disclosive power depending on where you are now on your journey with the Lord. Sometimes one story strikes home, sometimes another, depending on what he is doing in our hearts.

Mark 8:27-30 is that moment when Peter knows and is willing to say "You are the One."

> And Jesus went on with his disciples to the villages of Caesarea Philippi; and on the way he asked his disciples, "Who do men say that I am?" And they told him, "John the Baptist; and others say, Elijah; and others one of the prophets." And he asked them, "But who do you say that I am?" Peter answered him, "You are the Christ." And he charged them to tell no one about him.

At times I do see Jesus; I can say I believe in him, that he really is the Anointed One sent for me. But as verses 31-33 immediately bring out, Peter doesn't really understand this One in whom he believes, and neither do I.

> And he began to teach them that the Son of man must suffer many things, and be rejected by the elders and the chief priests and the scribes, and be killed, and after three days rise again. And he said this plainly. And Peter took him, and began to rebuke him. But turning and seeing his disciples, he rebuked Peter, and said, "Get behind me Satan! For you are not on the side of God, but of men."

The way of suffering and service is exactly the opposite of what Peter wants. Jesus' invitation cuts directly against the grain.

> And he called to him the multitude with his disciples, and he said to them, "If any man would come after me, let him deny himself and take up his cross and follow me. For whoever

would save his life will lose it; and whoever loses his life for my
sake and the gospel's will save it" (Mark 8:34-35).

The startling, frightening invitation is to leave one's very
self behind. To leave fishing nets is hard. To get out of the
boat that protects you from the chaos is terrifying. But to let
go of one's very self? Even to open my heart to think about it
brings me to the point where my life begins to dissolve. This
looks like death, and like Peter I want to run away.

Then, a little later, there is the vision at the top of the
mountain, unexpected, not really comprehended, just
given. Yet somehow, you know this is where it all goes.

And after six days Jesus took with him Peter and James and
John, and led them up a high mountain apart by themselves;
and he was transfigured before them, and his garments became
glistening, intensely white, as no fuller on earth could bleach
them. And there appeared to them Elijah with Moses; and they
were talking to Jesus. And Peter said to Jesus, "Master, it is well
that we are here; let us make three booths, one for you and one
for Moses and one for Elijah." For he did not know what to say,
for they were exceedingly afraid. And a cloud overshadowed
them, and a voice came out of the cloud, "This is my beloved
Son; listen to him." And suddenly looking around they no
longer saw anyone with them but Jesus only (Mark 9:2-8).

As I pray over this I, too, begin to catch a glimpse of the One
who is telling me that he is to be the Crucified One, and that
I am to follow in his way; but here I see him in his glory. For
a moment, unexpected, totally unearned, I see where it will
go. All one can say is, "Isn't it marvelous to be here." This
strengthens us; it heals our troubled hearts, to once again go
back and listen to Jesus with new courage and hope. "This is
my beloved Son; listen to him." And what has he been telling
us all along? Give over one's very self.

The moment of illumination keeps us moving, but as we
descend the mountain the day to day dullness takes over.

The image of our daily struggle to be faithful is:

> They were on the road, going up to Jerusalem; Jesus was walking ahead of them; they were in a daze, and those who followed were apprehensive. Once more taking the twelve aside he began to tell them what was going to happen. (Mark 10:32)

As I take this into my heart it reminds me so much of my life. Jesus knows where it is all going; but like the disciples in the story, I do not. I'm in a daze. I stumble along, not really seeing where I am going or why it has to be so difficult. But I see Jesus vaguely out before me, I hear him speak to me, and I keep going. This confused plodding, as I look at it through the prism of this story, begins to look like what faith is really like. Faith is being able to identify more and more with Peter, with his hopes, his generosity, his willingness to stumble along after Jesus, even with his blindness and betrayal. It is to recognize all of this as one's own. Eventually Peter was changed through all of this. What he could not see, what he had never wanted to see, he saw; he even thanked God for it. He really did let go of his very self. This gives me hope that the same transformation is going on in my heart and in yours.

This deep reading of these stories lets us begin to see how they are stories about you and me. There is the call and the gift of being enabled to spend our lives on a journey with Jesus where sometimes we understand, but mostly we don't. Sometimes we are unfaithful. Sometimes there is that glimpse at the top of the mountain which heals our hearts so that we can, in our own stumbling way, stay on the journey, though we can't say what it was except that it was good to be there. As we continue to follow him amid the tangled fidelities of our lives, he gradually makes us into what we need to be, fishers for the Kingdom.

Blindness

If we are at all honest with ourselves we have to admit that our attempts to journey with Jesus are often very confusing. Very often he seems so distant from us. Like the disciples in Mark 10:32 we seem to be in a daze, where we can barely see him. Something seems to cloud our vision. We grope after him in the darkness, hoping we have not lost him completely. In the depths of our hearts we begin to wonder if our faith can be very real. Because of this, to notice that the great journey at the heart of Mark's gospel is bracketed by two men who were blind, and who were healed, can come as an answer to prayer. They were blind too! Then Mark must have known; he is talking to me. And we go back to the stories with new insight, new hope, our hearts open to hear what the Lord has to say to us.

> And they came to Bethsaida. And some people brought to him a blind man, and begged him to touch him. And he took the blind man by the hand, and led him out of the village; and when he had spit on his eyes and laid his hands upon him, he asked him, "Do you see anything?"
> And he looked up and said, "I see men; but they look like trees, walking." Then again he laid his hands upon his eyes; and he looked intently and was restored, and saw everything clearly. And he sent him away to his home, saying, "Do not even enter the village" (Mark 8:22-26).

As we listen before this in silence, and go back to it time and again, we begin to wonder: "What is this blindness?" For in an intuitive way we know this blindness is our own. Here as we open ourselves to the Lord in the stillness of this story he is taking us by the hand and leading us out of it. First he starts to let us sense this blindness that traps us, for this is the beginning of our being healed.

If we look to the story that immediately precedes this one, we can see that though the twelve have been with Jesus, have heard him preach, seen his healing power, they cannot see the true meaning of the miraculous feeding of the four thousand. They cannot see in it the sign of the eschatological banquet. Jesus asks them "Do you not yet perceive or understand? Are your hearts hardened? Having eyes do you not see, and having ears do you not hear?" And the painful answer is "no." They cannot see it. And what is even more painful is that in the midst of the story I come to see that I can't see it either. As I turn these painful words over in my heart I go back to my own life and the promise of God's love that has been so often offered to me. How often that gift has been missed. Not rejected, but missed because I never even saw it. This unspeakable love of God for me has been there in the care and support of family and friends. I've taken it all for granted or I've passed through it so preoccupied that I scarcely ever opened my heart to the huge mystery that called me. But here it dawns on me and I can see much more clearly how I have always been his beloved.

Going back to the story another time teaches me other things. Meeting Jesus, hearing his call, has saved me from meaninglessness. But the reality of this slips away from me. I see others desperately searching for something to keep them going, hoping against hope that their drifting lives might go somewhere. I see the real terror that grips them, and forget that I have been freed from this desperation. I live so comfortably in my faith that the Father loves us all and that therefore our lives are eternally significant. This forgetfulness seeps into my heart and blinds me. Then there is the much more intimate matter of the call to deepening involvement with the One who loves me. The Lord's gentle but daily invitation to prayer, to deepening surrender, can be so quiet that the chatter of my life drowns out this fateful call. The result is that I have neglected my true destiny to be the Father's beloved. I blindly disregard the gift of his intimacy; I flounder in my own darkness, saying he is my Father by hardly responding as a beloved son. I rush through my prayers; or I put them off until tomorrow, only half realizing the consequences of the decision I so easily make.

Even when I am open to God's gift of his love in the people he sends into my life, or in the intimate stirrings of my own heart, I often forget that this is an other worldly love. We only glimpse it here; but that glimpse is enough to give us hope, to lead us on a voyage of faith where we will leave behind our old selfish ways. Precisely because this hope is so unlimited we are never quite going to possess it here. There will always be the poor and the hungry, those who have been brutalized and have become brutal or pathetic in return. There will always be misunderstanding and loneliness. At their best marriage and community are deep enough and whole enough to point beyond themselves, but at their worst they seem claustrophobic. And when the loneliness, and the fear, and the claustrophobia pile up, we can forget that we are called by an other worldly hope. Then we want it all now. In my own desperation I can look to "the leaven of the Pharisees and the leaven of Herod." Like them I can despair and turn away from this unspeakable hope. I can look for something else to fill my heart. Like the Pharisees I can turn to "keeping the rules," hoping in my own integrity, or respectability, a clear but torturous conscience to save me, to let me feel that I am somebody. Or like Herod I can look to power, pleasure, security, in the desperate gamble that they will give me what my heart needs. All of this is what blinds us.

If we look forward from the blindness of the man in Mark 8:22-26, it clearly points to the cross. Peter finally, with God's help, can see that Jesus is the Anointed One of God; but he cannot, he does not want to, see the cross. It is too horrifying. It cuts against the grain. It threatens and would dismantle the whole way he has constructed of looking at himself and the world, of making sense of his life. Like all of us, Peter has been born into a world that is overwhelming, and yet one in which he must find a safe place if he is to survive. Loneliness, confusion, a sense of his own fragility, but most of all the fear of his own death loom about him. Like every man he has to learn a way of dealing with these human dilemmas. Often enough we really don't know, or we can't let ourselves know, what the problem really is. It is too much for us to face. But we hit on an ingenious way of moving past it. For example we try to avoid death by being very popular, or by achieving something in our work of lasting significance. Because one or two times that helps us cope with the terror of oblivion, or seems to, we go back to it again and again. These attempts to escape become written into the way we live, so that we no longer even notice them. Hiding in these illusions we set out to protect ourselves. That self, as we see it, needs whatever pleasure it can get. It needs to be comfortable, to avoid whatever is painful or confusing. Sometimes it needs to avoid the true self's hunger for truth, because that would force it to face the lies it lives. Sometimes it won't let the true self's need to

surrender to God even surface, because this would
demolish its attempt to pretend that it is self-sufficient. This
is a pretense it hides in because it cannot face its destiny of
death. All of these are illusions that distort and submerge
the true self, the self who is the beloved of the Father; but at
the same time they allow the fabricated self—the self you
and I and Peter have constructed in our attempts to
survive—to keep functioning.

Jesus' cross challenges all of these illusions. The cross is
pain. It is defeat. It is the collapse of all of these false hopes.
The whole world we build around ourselves that cor-
responds to these illusions crumbles in the face of the cross.
Still the blindness that fosters these illusions can be very
subtle. I have gotten good at talking about the cross. I have
learned to compartmentalize my life and relegate the cross
to areas of my life where I can handle it, where it is not
too awkward. Or I discover a false cross that somehow fits
into and reinforces my illusions. Then I can go along as I
always have, but now with the pious support of the cross of
Jesus. This is very convenient. But Peter hasn't had time to
develop all of these smoke screens. The reality of it hits him
head on. For him it is truly horrifying. It is not just that it
would be difficult. It is that his whole way of living is being
struck out from under him. Any other way of living seems to
be literally unimaginable. As I slowly open my heart to this
story in faith, the Lord starts to get through to me. Just as in
the story, I gradually begin to see. I see how these things are
present in my life, how my illusions keep me going, how I
live off them, and how false they are. Here I experience the
same fear and panic that swept through Peter's heart. "This
would be to die; it would be the end of the very self I think I
am." But then in the midst of that terror, the Lord is present
gradually healing me. He grasps us deeper than our terrors

and somehow we let go of part of our old self as we cling to him. We hear the call of this gentle Jesus as he gradually strips us of our illusions and we go with him. But often this stripping seems to be anything but gentle.

The second healing from blindness comes at the very end of Jesus' journey to Jerusalem.

> And as he was leaving Jericho with his disciples and a great multitude, Bartimaeus, a blind beggar, the son of Timaeus, was sitting by the roadside. And when he heard that it was Jesus of Nazareth, he began to cry out and say, "Jesus, Son of David, have mercy on me!" And many rebuked him, telling him to be silent; but he cried out all the more, "Son of David, have mercy on me!" And Jesus stopped and said, "Call him." And they called the blind man, saying to him, "Take heart; rise, he is calling you." And throwing off his mantle he sprang up and came to Jesus. And Jesus said to him, "What do you want me to do for you?" "Master," the blind man answered, "Let me receive my sight." And immediately he received his sight and followed him on the way (Mark 10:46-52).

Of course, many of the same things come up again, but there are also some very important differences. In the earlier story, the blind man was brought to Jesus. Here, he hears Jesus is coming and painfully aware of his blindness he begins to cry out. The paradox is that this man can see how desperate his situation really is; and this grounds his resolve. He pushes aside as unimportant what others think. He cuts through the opposition of the fickle crowd. Nothing else counts but to get to Jesus who alone can heal him.

This brings out something new. Having listened to the other story, having come to the point where we are beginning to have a sense of our own blindness, when we enter into this story, we very quickly take Bartimaeus' words as our own. With a deep sense of our desperate state we cry out "Jesus, Son of David, have mercy on me!"

Then we hear the Lord saying, "What do you want me to do for you?" Here, again, it is crucial not just to have begun to understand Bartimaeus, but to have entered so deeply into the story that you become him. Then those words that we desperately need to hear, are addressed to you and me: "What do you want me to do for you?" The response that comes welling up out of our depths is "Master." Nor is this just politeness. It is who Jesus is becoming in my life and in yours. He is the master of the journey. Although I cannot see very well, I have been learning to follow him, to trust him, not my own illusions. Before we ran from pain. The result was that often our prayer was "don't let me be hurt." Here the request is "Heal me of this blindness," though at this point I know this will, indeed it already has, entailed a stripping.

There is another shift in this story as compared with the first one. Here the cure is instantaneous. In the first story the emphasis was on how Jesus gradually heals us of our blindness. Here the story points to the results of this healing. The blind man is freed to follow Jesus along the way, to join in his journey to Jerusalem, where Peter did not want to go. As we, in prayer, inhabit this story we know that the Lord is there healing us, bringing us with him on his journey, preparing us to embrace his cross.

Living within these stories can give us a very different way of looking at our lives. Our own disappointments, or the times we were drawn into the huge pain that touches those we love, can be seen in a new way. Haven't these turning points often been the times when Jesus has invited us to let go of our illusions and false hopes and go with him? Weren't these times when the Lord called us to go with him where our fears didn't want us to go, to leave behind what we thought we had to have if we were to survive? A lot of this pain and confusion in our lives, this dryness we experience in our efforts to be faithful, this crumbling of our old ways of protecting ourselves, this increasing ability to see the games we play, this is not just wasted pain, the home ground of cynicism. Seen from within these stories, we can begin to see some of it for what it is, the place where Jesus is stripping us of our illusions. Here Jesus is the Lord of our dis-illusionment, for he is freeing us from our illusions, and bringing us into the Kingdom of his Father. To come to see this lets us transform many of the painful facts of our lives into mysteries by discerning in them this saving encounter with the Lord.

Remembering

The second chapter of Luke presents us with a marvelous series of stories. As I think back these stories about the birth of Jesus seem to have always been a part of me. I can remember listening to them at home and in church when I was a little boy. And that's the aspect I'd like to focus on in these stories: the place of memory in the life of a religious person. This starts in verses 22-24 with a cultic act of remembering.

> And when the time came for their purification according to the law of Moses, they brought him up to Jerusalem to present him to the Lord (as it is written in the law of the Lord, "Every male that opens the womb shall be called holy to the Lord") and to offer a sacrifice according to what is said in the law of the Lord, "a pair of turtledoves, or two young pigeons" (Luke 2:22-24).

In their deep and direct faith the parents of Jesus do for him what the law required. As a first born son he must be redeemed, that is presented to the Lord as his own, and received back, recalling the deliverance of the Hebrew people from slavery in Egypt, when only the first born sons of those who had celebrated the first passover supper had been saved from death. In this act of remembering Jesus and his parents are caught up in that great event of Jewish history, of their history. Right then it is happening again within them, for Jesus is *the* first born Son, and what started ages before pointed to this day. Balancing this ritual form of remembering is a much more private form. Towards the end of the chapter we see Mary who "stored up all these things in her heart." Here we have the picture of Mary turning over in her heart these things about her son, going back to them, trying to penetrate their deep meaning. We see a heart open to the great mysteries of God's love playing through these events of her life. Both types of remembering were a part of Mary's way of being open to the mystery that surrounded her.

When I let these stories get at me, I know I have to follow Mary in this, but I scarcely know how to do it. So much of my life is running from one thing to the next that there is little time to reflect on what has and is happening to me, to be still and try to see the deep meaning to things. Even when there is time I tend to run from it in panic because I do not know how to deal with it. This kind of frenzy is a large part of the neurosis that grips my living and yours. One of the ways this works itself out is in a forgetfulness of our own history. I am hiding from my painful past; or I am out of touch with my deep but elusive past. Because of that I live in a fog. I really don't remember or understand where I came from, I can't see where I am now, and I drift vaguely into the future.

C. S. Lewis can jar us, provoking us to live in a less forgetful way. In *Out of the Silent Planet*,[1] which is the first volume of his space trilogy, his hero, Dr. Ransom, has wound up on Mars and is having a conversation with Hyoi, who is a *hross*. They are talking about pleasure and man's need for it, indeed his selfishness in seeking it.

Ransom says:

"Is the begetting of young not a pleasure among the *hrossa*?" (*Hrossa* is the plural form of *hross*.)
"A very great one, *Hman*. (*Hman* is the hross word for man).

This is what we call love."

"If a thing is a pleasure, a *hman* wants it again. He might want the pleasure more often than the number of young that could be fed." It took Hyoi a long time to get the point.

"You mean," he said slowly, "that he might do it not only in one or two years of his life but again?"

"Yes."

"But why? Would he want his dinner all day or want to sleep after he had slept? I do not understand."

"But a dinner comes every day. This love, you say, comes only once while the *hross* lives?"

"But it takes his whole life. When he is young he has to look for his mate; and then he has to court her; then he begets young; then he rears them; then he remembers all this, and boils it inside him and makes it into poems and wisdom."

"But the pleasure he must be content only to remember?"

"I do not understand. A pleasure is full grown only when it is remembered. You are speaking, *Hman*, as if the pleasure were one thing and the memory another. It is all one thing . . . . When you and I met, the meeting was over very shortly, it was nothing. Now it is growing something as we remember it. But still we know very little about it. What it will be when I remember it as I lie down to die, what it makes in me all my days till then—that is the real meeting. The other is only the beginning of it. You say you have poets in your world. Do they not teach you this?"

This can get us going. His suggestion that we only gradually come to a true realization of what has happened to us, and that really it hasn't finished until we have spent our whole lives mulling it over and discovering what that has meant, how it has changed us down through the years, rings true with me. It brings me back to Luke's gospel and the stories I have known since I was a little boy. When you and I start to listen to these stories about Jesus and Mary in this new light, then we begin to see that these events were not over and done with right there. They keep changing and developing as Jesus and Mary turn them over in their hearts. This means the exodus wasn't over and done with in 1200 B.C., or whenever it happened. It reverberates right down to the presentation of this first Son. Its real meaning keeps unfolding. No one in 500 B.C., then, could possibly understand the full significance of the exodus, simply because it was still unfolding. And when Jesus, as the gospels tell us, took up that same passover memorial and interpreted his death in terms of it, that unfolding reached a new stage. But the mystery is still unfolding in history as you and I and countless others are infolded into it. As you and I begin to remember this in the story, the Lord is drawing us into his huge mystery. We can sense something of how all of this is my history and yours. The first born Son draws us into his destiny, and his mother and her deep way of remembering is a model for us.

The image of Mary turning things over in her heart points me toward my own history. She invites me to discover for myself that the deepest truth of events is only revealed gradually. Their effect is worked in us over a long period and their real meaning keeps unfolding. If I am to be in touch with them I have to keep remembering them; I have to keep turning them over in my heart. As I listen to Mary doing this in the story my mind starts to wander back over my own journey. I think of the time recently when I was with two friends and we were listening to the radio as it played the hit tunes from past years. The year 1962 came up and to their huge merriment I off-handedly remarked, "Oh, that was the year I finally decided that Camus was wrong after all." That brought me back to one of the turning points of my religious life. At that time I was struggling towards adult faith. The possibility that we were all alone in the universe was terrifyingly real, as was the deep hope that all I had been taught about God was true. That afternoon sitting in my room is still so clear to me, when I realized I really did believe, and that I had to give my whole heart to this Father who loved us. But it is only now, as I remember that, as I have so often returned to it and my final resolution of it, that I can see the pivotal stance of that in my life. Indeed, it was only gradually that I came to see all those difficulties as the hidden but real graces they were. And yet that final resolution is not a dead thing. It is part of me. In a real sense it is me, and it is still unfolding. By remembering it and its continuing life in me I can start to see what is at the very heart of my life, and where and how God moves me.

Listening to this story another time I am reminded of a time in college when I stood at a railroad station waiting for a train to take me home, and in God's wisdom my whole world fell apart and was put back together, all in a moment. Then there is a flood of memories. I recall the gentleness of my father after I had ruined one of the family cars and I told him how sorry I was; and all he ever said was, "I knew you would be." Then there was that time in the seminary when I was given a copy of *Seeds of the Desert* by Rene Voillaume. His call to follow Jesus was so stark that I couldn't go with him, but it rang so true that I couldn't let it go either. It shattered my comfortable little world, only to become the book I lived on for eight years. Now I try to share it with my students. Or there was a friend's invitation to start reading John of the Cross. Gradually all these events start to form a pattern, the pattern of my life. As I recall them I start to see the journey of my own life unfolding through all of it, and I'm caught by the sheer grace of it. This kind of prayerful remembering allows you to see what you couldn't see at the time, namely these struggles, these decisions and risks, the people you met, these were not just accidents. Only later on, as you carefully recall your elusive past, can you start to see what was really happening. As you see it you are free to accept it more fully and enter into it more completely. Just as Hyoi knew that he could only see the full import of his meeting with Ransom as he remembered it at his death, so I cannot yet see the full meaning of my baptism and ordination. Their real significance is still unfolding, and I won't be able to see them in their fullness until I look back and remember it all as I die. All of this is caught up in the still unfolding meaning of the exodus and resurrection, and in my remembering I see flashes of that.

Then there comes the time when you begin to see that your friends are doing the same thing. They, too, are constantly going back over the events of their lives as they more and more attempt to come to grips with their journeys and the way God has been working in them, weaving together their failures and sacrifices into a life of faith. When you start to share that you get a deeper insight into how unique each story is, but you also start to see the parallels. As you listen to your friends it starts to dawn on you, "But that was like the time . . .," or you think, "That's what that meant." You see your own life illumined in the experience of the others. Getting a deeper sense of the journeys your friends have been on helps you remember your own more accurately. In seeing their lives, and the mystery of it, and seeing how God was gracious there, and time again in one's own life, we learn to live in the present with deeper hope and trust. We have a deeper sense of God's presence in our lives and even when we can't understand what is happening we are more able to trust, as we recall how risk has been transformed into gift in the past. We are learning to live the way Mary did.

This remembering can be very awkward when it brings us back to our painful past. Then we have to learn to forgive the past, not forgetting but remembering differently. Many people live with great scars. They feel they have been betrayed, harmed, perhaps irreparably, by family, their education, their religious formation, their nation. These events of their past have estranged them from others, from life itself; and they are deeply resentful of the things that were done to them. Sometimes they are also ashamed and angry with themselves that they let this happen. Very often the result is that they cannot let the past go. They do not forget it but bury it deeply within, where it smolders. They brood. The ancient wrongs keep destroying the present. This is killing, for it lets the evil of the past unfold into the present and continue to contaminate their lives.

Our hearts need to be freed; these devastatingly painful memories need to be healed. This would be a liberation for which we desperately long. But how? In these stories Mary gives us a hint. Living within this story, I can't help but think that Simeon's prophecy that, "A sword will pierce through your own soul," stayed with Mary; and her confusion over the losing and finding of Jesus in the Temple was a premonition for her. In my own confusion and dismay I try to open my heart to her heart beneath the cross. How did she open herself to the mystery of God's love even in the shattering events of her life? I don't know. But I know from her that I, too, have to learn this kind of simplicity that leads to real wisdom. Somehow the figure of Jacob comes to mind.

Jacob was a crafty, sometimes ruthless, sometimes cowardly man who thought he knew exactly what he wanted out of life: a beloved wife, sons, land, posterity. But as you work into the story you start to sense that God is working something even deeper in Jacob's life, something that transcends the human vision, and certainly the goodness of Jacob himself. The invitation given again and again to Jacob

is to trust in God so much that he would hand over the
control in his life, especially in the areas of his chief
concerns, to God. This is precisely what he is reluctant to do.
Time and again his fears and insecurities, his cunning and
deception, push him to seize control. He tricks his brother.
He fools his father and lies to him. He is always calculating,
scheming to get what he wants, desperately hanging on to
what he has already gotten. He fights with his brother and
father; he tangles with his uncle; his wives and sons are
caught up in it. He even wrestles with God. That seems to be
the underlying theme. Jacob does love and trust his God;
but he also wants to control his own life. He is afraid to let
God really take over. So he fights him. This has to remind us
of ourselves; we, too, wrestle with our God.

Looking at the same story, but from the perspective of
what God is doing allows us to see it quite differently. God
takes the mixed up events, even the sins, and writes them
into his story. Jacob lies to his father and fools him and in
that way receives the blessing intended for his brother. But
the blessing is given and it abides. Because of that he has to
leave home. That leads him to where he is tricked by his
uncle Laban. That in turn is taken up by God and written
into the story. The rivalry between Leah and Rachel leads to
Jacob's fathering twelve sons, and they become the twelve
tribes of Israel. Even the treachery of the sons against
Joseph leads, in God's wisdom, to their salvation. Still much,
if not all of this, is beyond Jacob's vision. When his sons
come back from Egypt asking for Benjamin, Joseph's full
brother and the old man's joy, as he thinks, the only
remaining son of his beloved Rachel, he doesn't want to let
him go. He doesn't want to lose him. He cannot see that not
only will he not lose him, but he will get Joseph back as well.
God has to force him out of his grip.

When Jacob finally comes to Egypt there is a great scene as he meets his long lost Joseph.

> Joseph had his chariot made ready and went up to meet his father Israel (Jacob) in Goshen. As soon as he appeared he threw his arms around his neck and for a long time wept on his shoulder. Israel said to Joseph, "Now I can die, now that I have seen you again, and seen you still alive" (Genesis 46:29-30).

Letting these words seep into me I begin to wonder if there hasn't finally been a great change in Jacob. Seeing Joseph and all of his sons, he finally seems to see how God has been faithful all along. He can finally catch something of the careful way God has always been with him. Here at the end of his life he can look back on it and be reconciled to it. He can stop fighting.

After Jacob dies and is laid to rest with his forefathers, Joseph's brothers come to him.

> His brothers came themselves and fell down before him. "We present ourselves before you," they said, "as your slaves." But Joseph answered them, "Do not be afraid; is it for me to put myself in God's place? The evil you planned to do me has by God's design been turned to good, that he might bring about, as indeed he has, the deliverance of a numerous people. So you need not be afraid; I myself will provide for you and your descendants." In this way he reassured them with words that touched their hearts (Genesis 50:18-20).

Joseph is so simple that he can see the deep things of God. He doesn't forget what has happened—even how his brothers betrayed him—but he can forgive the past and in that he is free to see this deeper truth. As we open our hearts to Mary and this Joseph, son of Jacob, we are being invited to live in the same deep way: forgiving the past, not forgetting, but remembering differently. It was Mary's sense of being loved that let her do this, and it seems that this was also present in Joseph's life. This seems to have dawned on Jacob when he finally saw his lost son, freeing him to stop fighting. As we inhabit these stories we too begin to sense that it is the One who loved them who also loves us and who invites us to open our hearts to forgive the past as they did.

[1]C.S. Lewis, *Out of the Silent Planet*. N.Y.: Macmillan. The section I will quote comes from pp. 72-73.

The Way of Powerlessness

One way of looking at chapters eighteen and nineteen of St. John's gospel is to see them as a conviction of power. In one scene after another Jesus stands alone before an angry mob, the whole retinue of corrupt religious power, the brutal power of an empire, ultimately he stands before the power of death. He never hides from the dark side of power. He confronts it with his simple honesty and his trust in his Father. What we see lived out in Jesus is the firm belief that the kingdom and the power and the glory are the Father's. Wavering between the calm, resolute, power-filled stance of Jesus as he chooses to stand powerless before the men of power, Annas and Pilate, and Judas' giving into the allure of power, stands Peter.

In the stories it is clear that Peter wants to follow Jesus; but like us he is so afraid. He needs Jesus. He desperately needs the deep way of life Jesus incarnates. He needs to trust in God, be simple and loyal. He longs to be faithful. He also needs to hide a lot. Many things frighten him. Powerful people make him feel small. But he still wants them to like him. Disgrace, loneliness and death he can't face at all. The mixture of all of these things in his heart leads to his inconsistent behavior. One minute he is makng a great show, striking off the ear of the servant of the High Priest; the next he is so frightened that he can't even bring himself to admit he knows Jesus to a little serving girl. Still, this confusing behavior is not unknown to us, for as we inhabit these stories we can once again see how much we are like Peter. If "perfect love banishes fear" (1 Jn. 4:18) then it is clear that Peter's love and my love are not perfect. I easily get afraid, and then I grab for something to make me strong. Like Peter I look to power.

Holding these images in my heart I start to get glimpses into what is in my heart. Peter and you and I live with huge needs. We need to be understood, accepted, loved. We desperately need to know we are worthwhile, and cherished. But these authentic needs can be distorted and then I'll go after mere security, pleasure, power. In either case I cannot satisfy these needs on my own. I go out to others. When I get desperate I am forced into a position of depending on others for these things. Then I don't go out to the others free to love and understand them, inviting the same gift in return. I go out to get what I need to escape my weakness. Here I live half strangled by fears. I fear these powerful others on whom I must depend. I fear I am not really loved or esteemed; I doubt I am worthwhile. I begin to wonder if somewhere, somehow, I haven't done something utterly terrible that has left me tarnished, though I'm not at all sure what it could be. I fear the support and attention I so desperately need will be taken away. Here I tend to panic. In the midst of this indemic insecurity I reach out to manipulate people and situations to get what I feel I need. In this fear I both accept, even greedily seek out, what I want; but I also resent those to whom I go. This is a deep but unseen distortion cutting me off from the mutual understanding and love for which my heart was made. Sometimes this becomes written so deeply into us that we become trapped in our pathetic weakness.

In these stories Peter is baffled, confused and finally

terribly threatened. That's when he panics. This weakness traps him, pulling him away from that for which he really longs. Peter seems to have an inkling of this, and even after the disaster in the garden this draws him on to the High Priest's house. As I turn these frightening stories over in my heart I, too, sense there is something here. Still, like Peter I find Jesus' free and consistent choice to be powerless more than I can bear. Somewhere, it attacks me. Because of that Peter and I respond not just with incomprehension, though there is an element of that, but with violent rejection. I start out distorting what Jesus is saying and doing because I look at him through the eyes of my fear and pathetic weakness. Then I have to reject what he says and does to protect myself. "No one could live like that," I tell myself. "After all, you have to be realistic." But saying this within these stories rings hollow. I can tell there is something false about it.

I begin to remember other stories in the gospels where Jesus' stark simplicity stands revealed, other instances where he seems to speak of a strength that comes from freely choosing to be powerless.

> And they were bringing children to him, that he might touch them; and the disciples rebuked them. But when Jesus saw it he was indignant, and said to them, "Let the children come to me, do not hinder them; for to such belongs the Kingdom of God. Truly, I say to you, whoever does not receive the Kingdom of God like a child shall not enter it." And he took them in his arms and blessed them, laying his hands upon them.
> (Mark 10:13-16)

This means much more than the simple fact that Jesus was fond of little children. Holding it in my heart, going back to it day after day, I gradually see it as one of Jesus' paradoxes. It is one of those simple little sayings or actions that seems so tame until one day it comes alive to turn reality on its ear.

Jesus' consistent call throughout the gospels is to adult decision, to take the awful responsibility for one's own life. This is precisely what little children cannot do. In all things that really matter they have to depend on others. What then does Jesus mean when he says, "Whoever does not receive the Kingdom of God like a child shall not enter it"? What is he saying to me? Surely, this is the Lord's invitation to admit that ultimately I cannot save myself. I can do many things for myself; but in all the decisive things, life, death, a meaning to existence, I have to depend on him. Freed by my trust in him and his Father's love, I can face that; indeed I can freely choose to put aside all pretense that I can do for myself and confidently entrust all my hope in him. I can freely decide to be the Father's little one. This is the paradox: that someone who really had a sense of their own worth, who could deal with other people, who in a multiplicity of ways was strong, resourceful, who could face the awful responsibility for his own life, should freely choose not to rely on that but on the Father's love alone. This is the way into the kingdom.

With this paradox echoing in my heart, the beatitudes come back to me. If I could live in this paradox, if I really could see and accept my utter dependence; more, if strengthened by God's love I could rejoice that I was called to seek all my safety in my beloved Father, then I could come home to the beatitudes. If I could freely choose to rely on the Father, in childlike simplicity, I could afford to be poor because I wouldn't be hiding from my weakness in riches. I would have already dealt with that in handing myself over to my Father. I could be free to embrace the sorrow and confusion of others because he had strengthened me to do so. I could be meek with the powerful because my security would not come from them but from my Father. This would be so because in my own way I had done what Jesus had done before me, done for me: handed over his life and even his death to his Father.

The love that the beloved Father lavishes on us heals us of our enfeebling weakness, a weakness that so terrorizes us that we seek to grasp at power and security wherever we can find them. Swamped by our own weakness we cling to money, position, pleasure, power, even blatant injustice, indeed anything that might offer escape. This is the very opposite of the beatitudes. But the hope, the challenge of the beatitudes is: how blessed is the man or woman freed to live beyond all of that, freed to live in the kingdom. As I come back again to chapters eighteen and nineteen I can feel how I, too, am being called to live in that kingdom, to choose to trust only in the power of the Father. This liberation is radically dependent on the free gift of the Father's love, but it also calls for a decision on our part. The Father's love pouring into our hearts opens them up so that we can leave behind these false saviors, if we choose to. But this choice is experienced as a wrenching. As the Spirit drew Jesus out into the desert of choice after his baptism, so these stories bring to speech the invitation that is addressed to me, drawing me into the desert of renunciation and decision.

This is a land of disaffection. It is hard to leave behind comfort and selfish dreams to follow Jesus. More than that is asked of us now. Here we have to leave behind the very stratagems we use to protect ourselves. It may be a false self we are protecting, but it is the self we feel we are and desperately sense we have to defend. This fragile self has clothed itself with ways of acting that seemed innocent or at least necessary. There is the habitual inclination to use one's gifts to draw attention to the self, and there is the darker danger of collaborating in the dominion of evil. The temptation is to accept the often brutal use of power in the world, to begin to align one's self with it even in little ways. To override or disregard others by a show of one's gifts or one's ruthlessness, to thoughtlessly exploit the advantage age or position bring, to carefully manipulate instead of being simple and forthright. To abandon these ingrained ways of acting is to leave one's self vulnerable, undefended. This is more than scary.

The gospels tell us that Jesus was attacked in the desert. But when he came out of the desert he was ready. In story after story we see that he was a man who knew that he was the beloved of the Father and who chose to rely on that and not on whatever power or security he could create or discover for himself. Grounded in his Father's love, imaginative, capable of deep human intimacy and fidelity, blessed with charismatic gifts, he chose to proclaim the miracle of his Father's love in utter simplicity. This is a man who is strong. He knows who he is and what he will do. He does not hide from his Father or from himself and so he doesn't need to hide from others. He invites people into fellowship with him; but he never manipulates them. If they choose to open their hearts to him and his Father, he rejoices; if they choose to go another way, he lets them go. But he does not stop loving them. He is not defensive. He has it out with the Pharisees time and again, but he still keeps listening for the honest question, the open and sincere heart. He is himself with rich and poor, prostitute and pious Jew. He can weep over Jerusalem because he loves her, and yet challenge her for the same reason. This is not a weak man, someone who is powerless because he is pathetic. This is a man who has chosen to trust in his Father's power and in nothing else, so that when men and women follow him it is not because they are awed by his power, or dazzled by his miracles, but because the miracle of his Father's love has broken into their hearts with its startling strangeness and healed them. In his daily actions he constantly reaffirms his choice of the way of powerlessness.

This is something of what we see in chapters eighteen and nineteen. When the mob comes to get him, knowing exactly what he is doing, he meets them with the simple, "I am he." They recoil. When he is taken before the High Priest he does not pretend or try to hide. He cuts through the maneuvering and calmly takes his stand on his word. Caiphas doesn't quite know what to do. Before Pilate this reversal of who is really strong is even starker. Pilate has the soldiers, but it is Jesus who is steadfast. Pilate gives in to pressure, for power is his god; Jesus quietly holds fast to the path of powerlessness he entered when he left the desert. Before the last power, death, he is faithful to his Father. He gives away his life.

As I open my heart to these stories, letting them reverberate within me, and as you do the same, aren't we aware that we are being called to follow our master in this too? Jesus certainly wasn't naive. He knew what was in men's hearts. He saw clearly what was coming. But he never looked to power to protect himself. Out of this seems to come Jesus' admonition to his disciples to "be wise as serpents and innocent as doves" (Mt. 10:17). As these stories sink into us this call becomes tangible; and we are brought face to face with the times and places where we embrace power, times when we go along with others without really wondering where the truth lies, places where we don't listen but try to dominate. We remember with remorse all sorts of things, some little, others much more devastating, when to protect ourselves or to get our way, or just out of habit, we hid in power. These stories force us to admit that here we hand ourselves over to the power of darkness. This is part of our refusal to really trust in the Father the way Jesus did. It is a refusal to enter into the intimacy Jesus shared with his Father, where he knew he was loved and understood by his Father, and gave over his whole heart in return. That intimacy was at the center of his being and it gave him the strength to stand innocently and gently unbowed before the men of power. Here in these stories he calls you and me to follow in his way, to open our hearts to his Father and, relinquishing our futile attempts to prop ourselves up, to let his Father do it.

Really it is no accident that Jesus consistently chose to be powerless. It is part of his eschatological mission, for it clearly makes manifest that the only real power is the power of the Father. This is startling, confusing, because it embodies the great reversal, the turning inside out and upside down of all human expectation. Gently, sometimes abruptly, the Lord is challenging us to abandon our attempts to seize power and control. He is inviting us to freely choose to hand over the control of our lives to the Father with childlike simplicity. The invitation goes even beyond this. We are called to deal with people from the midst of this simplicity as Jesus did, where there is no hidden agenda, where we are not naive, where we choose to live without grasping at power, and in that invite others to do the same.

Guilt and Sin

We can read the gospels for years without noticing that they are filled with deeply flawed people, men blinded by selfishness, paralyzed by fear, women caught in adultery or pestering Jesus that he would give her sons the first places in his kingdom. There are lepers, prostitutes, cheats and betrayers. We see Jesus meet them, love them, and send them on healed. This we accept. But we find it so hard to believe it about ourselves. Something seems to block it. We stay trapped by our own dark side, while we quickly gloss over the fears and selfishness of the people we see on every page of the gospels. If we could find out what this block was and face it, perhaps that would let us know the healing love of the Lord.

Suppose we were to take one of these stories to ourselves, stepping into it so that it came alive in our hearts. Perhaps as we entered into the stance of the person in the story we could find out not only how much he or she is like us, but also see what it is in us that blocks us off from the healing touch of Jesus.

Early in the morning he came again to the temple; all the people came to him, and he sat down and taught them. The scribes and pharisees brought a woman who had been caught in adultery, and placing her in the midst they said to him, "Teacher, this woman has been caught in the act of adultery. Now in the law Moses commanded us to stone such. What do

you say about her?" This they said to test him, that they might
have some charge to bring against him. Jesus bent down and
wrote with his finger on the ground. And as they continued to
ask him, he stood up and said to them, "Let him who is without
sin among you be the first to throw a stone at her." And once
more he bent down and wrote with his finger on the ground.
But when they heard it, they went away, one by one, beginning
with the eldest, and Jesus was left alone with the woman
standing before him. Jesus looked up and said to her, "Woman,
where are they? Has no one condemned you?" She said, "No
one, Lord." And Jesus said, "Neither do I condemn you; go,
and do not sin again" (John 8:1-11).

I can immediately identify with the woman; and as I enter
into the story I enter into her, and her experience easily
becomes my own. In fact, her experience awakens me to
what has been happening in my depths but what I could not
or did not know how to face. I feel myself being dragged out
into the open doing something intimately wrong. My
loneliness, my desperate need for affection, are there for all
to see. How their eyes pierce me, peering into me,
examining my shame, my squandered integrity.

Then they leave me there, standing alone in the middle;
and I am isolated in my loneliness and shame. I'm cut off
from all those standing safely around me. A huge door
seems to be slamming shut, cutting me off from family and
friends as I wonder in agony, "What will they think?" And
God? I can't even look at him. I would hide from them all,
but there is nowhere to go where their staring eyes will not
seek me out. Then the accusation of their eyes finds words,
"This woman has been caught in the act of adultery." That
action was unacceptable; she is unacceptable. I hear this
accusation and ingest this vision of myself. I make it my own.
I am guilty. That is my true reality. Welling up from my
depths is a voice that accepts the verdict of my accusers. It is
not just that I have done something wrong, something

shameful. I *am* wrong. This brooding sense that all I am is flawed, stained, overwhelms me. This makes me defenseless against the cruel, brutal words and glances that attack me. I'm defenseless because I accept their accusation. I'm cut off from God and others, trapped in my isolation, because I'm not worthy of them. I'm brought face to face with the sense of being not just unnecessary and unneeded, but unwanted, indeed radically unacceptable in my very self. Somehow there is something I have done or overlooked or something wrong with me that makes me unacceptable and that comes out in the terrible things I do. Even when I manage to keep it covered up, as I desperately try to do, it is there at the heart of me. What this is, I'm not quite sure. But I accept this terrible verdict of the pharisees as true and I live under this intolerable burden.

I look at their smug faces and know they are not interested in me, in my pain, my present humiliation and fear or the quiet desperation that has brought me here. They don't care about the burden I have tried to carry. I'm so beaten that I can't even protest against this. They are not interested in me, though my life is in jeopardy; I am only here so they can get at Jesus. Meanwhile Jesus sits there silently. He is the guiltless One. In his presence I am torn. I desperately want him to understand and love me so that this terrible guilty loneliness in which I'm dying will be broken. But if I let him see what I'm really like, won't he have to reject me? For a moment I'm tempted to lash out at him, in a desperate act of self-preservation to turn the accusation back on him. "You're a fraud; you don't love us. You only make us wallow in guilt." But then I listen to his silence. As the story that I am living makes clear, Jesus' silence does not accuse. In the silence he gently reaches out to the poor woman and now to me. He turns aside the accusations that

are breaking me. One by one they go away, beginning with
the oldest. At the end I am alone with him. As I stand there
before him, the accusations falling away from me, I am
changed. I am brought to see that I have been mistaken all
along. I am not unnecessary or unneeded. Most of all I am
not unacceptable. Who I am is only dawning on me in his
silence and under his gaze. I am acceptable to him. I am his
beloved. Then he sends me. But the one sent is hardly the
one who was dragged in before, for the one who is sent is
one who knows he is cherished and has been firmly
admonished not to betray that call to be loved and loving.
Nor are these mere words, for Jesus' love has healed me, has
freed me from the terrible accusation that I am
unacceptable. He has revealed to me who I really am: his
beloved who is sent into the world.

Being loved and being sent are not two separate things.
Ultimately they are one reality. Living within this story
brings me to the point where I start to see this in one gospel
story after another. For example, the disciples are called
into fellowship with Jesus and become fishers of men, which
means they are loved and sent. Jesus says to Peter and
Andrew, "Come with me, and I will make you fishers of
men" (Mk. 1:17). After the resurrection Jesus meets a
distraught Mary Magdalen in the garden, heals her with his
tender love and then tells her, "Go to my brothers, and tell
them that I am ascending to my Father and your Father, my
God and yours" (Jn. 20:17). Indeed, this identity of being
loved with being sent, which is the disciples' ultimate
identity, finds its radiant symbol in Jesus, the beloved Son
sent into the world. We saw something of this before when
we looked at Jesus' baptism. At the heart of the good news is
the joyful proclamation that Jesus is who you and I are
called to be. He is the Father's beloved sent for us; we are

called to be, in Jesus, the Father's beloved sons and daughters sent for the kingdom. The tragedy is that guilt blocks this.

This is what I discover in the midst of the story. Stepping into the place of the woman, at first I am flooded by a pervasive sense of myself as being unacceptable. Here I come to see that the guilty feelings that I experience when I do, or don't do, something are only a surface manifestation of a much deeper reality. They are occasions when I feel bad about what I do; but the root of this is the habitually negative way I feel about who I am. This primordial sense of being guilty proceeds and itself colors these actions, indeed all actions. Another might forgive me for the things I have done; but this forgiveness will come up against this primordial guilt and founder.[1] It cannot break through to free me from my deepest guilt because it never reaches the root of the problem, not what I have done but what I feel I am. On this deeper level I feel perpetually cut off from others and trapped in my own suffocating darkness. Even the presence of Jesus is painful. I experience him as an enigma, as a threat to my guilty life. At first he only makes me feel more guilty, awakening long forgotten and hardly recognized guilt. In the jaws of this guilt I cannot believe he could accept me and so I hide from the one who is what I desperately need to be and can never see myself becoming, the guiltless One, beloved of the Father. I burrow deeper into my own distorted way of living. In a desperate act of self-preservation I am on the brink of turning the accusation I feel on him. I am about to make the pharisees' attack my own. "He's a fraud. He's not holy. He is the sinner; he betrays us." Here I can see something of why they had to kill him. The guiltless One is made guilty for our sake. He dies condemned as unacceptable before God and man, hung on a tree, so that guilty men can feel safe. This is the great lie.[2] Just in time the gentle silence of the story where Jesus reaches out to cherish this poor woman touches my heart and this desperate attempt at self-defense falls away. "I don't have to protect myself against him." In a moment he sets my frightened heart free. The lie is exposed. I'm not guilty; I'm loved.

Guilt is experienced here as more than a moral category. It is a metaphysical cancer that eats into my very being. It is an obsessive mood which is virtually identical with a deep and paralyzing forlornness which excludes, or rather repels, human and divine acceptance because it immobilizes us within the conviction that we are unacceptable not just in some of our actions, but in our very being.[3] Such indemic guilt, unless it is shattered, renders the past and the future unredeemable and the present a never-ending wasteland filled with accusation. Living within this story can shatter this deep guilt. Here I am brought face to face with what I have always dreaded was true, and Jesus' love exposes it as the terrible lie it is. This opens up to me so many of the gospel stories that I have understood with my mind but never believed in my heart. I can hear Jesus telling his disciples that the kingdom is like a father who had two sons. In a way that is startlingly new I can see bits of myself in both sons. But most of all I can see the Father coming out to greet me, tears streaming down his face, his arms out to embrace me. I can hear him say to me, "This my son was dead, and is alive again; he was lost, and is found" (Lk. 15:24). It happens within my heart. I have been dead. That is the only word I can find for my old guilty life. But now the Father has found me and his love and acceptance has brought me back to life.

To speak of sin is to enter a radically different universe. To discover that I am a sinner is to be overwhelmed by the awareness that I am the beloved of the Father and so called, even opened up, to be a lover, and to see how I cover that over and betray it. This happens to me inside the stories. I experience in a new way how the Lord has always loved me, how he has reached out to heal me and I have subverted that gift. Even now I can see so clearly how I betray this gift of being loved and its invitation to be loving. The woman caught in adultery was healed and sent to share that healing love. So often it stays locked up inside me. This gives me some insight into why the saints confess that they are such great sinners while we, who are not saints, are perplexed by this and find ourselves saying things like, "I may not be great, but I'm not the worst person in the world." Then we wonder what on earth the saints could be talking about. What seems to have happened is that this abiding sense of being cherished by God has sunk deeper and deeper in them. As this happened it gradually displaced the fear and guilt that had distorted them. This is a process of integration and simplification. They gradually came to see themselves as they really were. This deep sense of being loved allowed them to see what they had always avoided seeing: the ingrained refusal to trust God and hand themselves over to him, the games they played with others and themselves.

This sense of being a sinner is the result of God's love working in our hearts. It is his love that opens up our hearts to see what we really are, and that strengthens us to endure the pain of seeing it. Because of this the discovery that I am a sinner is not oppressive, because the care of the Father for me, his sinner, is the dominant reality.[4] The Father's love crashes through on me to free me from my deep guilt and teach me true humility. This is a gift of terrible beauty.

Living within these stories discloses a double paradox. The sense of myself as being unacceptable so distorts my being, so fills me with accusation against myself and all reality that I cannot see myself as loved. The result of that is that I can never see myself as a sinner, as one who subverts that gift. Yet it is precisely this haunting sense of being guilty that makes the sinful act where I reject my real destiny as called and sent, something that comes naturally to me. The other side of this is the paradoxical liberation that comes from realizing that I am the Father's sinner.

[1]See Sebastian Moore, *The Crucified Jesus Is No Stranger*. N.Y.: Seabury Press, 1977, p. 106.

[2]This is developed at greater length in Moore's excellent book.

[3]Moore, p. 109.

[4]This is the experience in the earlier stages of our conversion. As John of the Cross makes clear there are times when very advanced souls have a different experience. Cf. *Dark Night*, II, 5, 5.

Waiting

Like each of the gospels, Luke tells us the story of John the Baptist.[1] As I open my heart to it I am struck by the waiting. Zechariah and Elizabeth had waited for a child until they had given up hope. Then Zechariah had to wait for nine months before he could say how God had blessed him and Elizabeth and in them all of Israel. Their son, John, seems to have spent his whole life, his whole religious life, waiting. His prophetic message was a call to others to join him in waiting, to learn to wait in fidelity for the God who was coming.

Reflected against the clarity of this story, I start to look at myself in a new way. I begin to notice how much of my life I spend waiting. I remember lying in bed as a little boy on Christmas eve, waiting for Santa Claus to come, praying that I would fall asleep soon, otherwise I'd just die from excitement. I think of how I wait for friends, of how I sometimes wait, wondering where my life will lead me. I wait in patience while I watch the students I teach grow from boys to men, for that takes time and I must know how to wait with them, if I am to help them. As I pray over these stories I know I am being called to see a great mystery of God's love in this waiting. It is not just wasting time. I am being invited to see this as a part of my journey. I have to learn to wait in faith like John the Baptist.

John seems to have begun his journey waiting in hope.

And the child grew and became strong in spirit, and he was in
the wilderness till the day of his manifestation to Israel.
(Luke 1:80)

Here I picture John called away from home, from friends,
out into a wilderness of solitude. This is not a burdensome
journey. It is difficult, but filled with huge hope. Something
is stirring in his heart that draws him to the desert, into a
wilderness where he does not yet possess his heart's desire
but is filled with hope. This image of John heading into the
wilderness of solitude reminds me that there is a loneliness
and a corresponding hope in me that cannot be reached
even by intimacy with other human beings. I need to be
touched by God, to see all of creation transformed. I know I
have been called into this expectant wilderness in the past
and the call echoes once again in my heart now. I have to
wait for him. Here my sense is that God is out before me,
and he calls me into his future where my heart will know
him. Gladly I journey into the wilderness waiting for him to
come.

. . .the word of God came to John the son of Zechariah in the
wilderness; and he went into all the region about the Jordan,
preaching a baptism of repentance for the forgiveness of sins.
As it is written in the book of the words of Isaiah the prophet,
"The voice of one crying in the wilderness:
Prepare the way of the Lord,
make his paths straight.
Every valley shall be filled,
and every mountain and hill shall be brought low,
and the crooked shall be made straight,
and the rough ways shall be made smooth;
and all flesh shall see the salvation of God."
(Luke 3:2-6)

John did not wait in vain. He left behind much; he journeyed into a wilderness, and there, filled with expectation, he waited for God. And God spoke to him. Sometimes this happens to you and me. We say our prayers; we do what we think God is calling us to; we wait hoping he will come into our hearts transforming our lives. Years of this simple, faithful, living slide by and then one day, as we go to mass or do our work, we have a quiet sense that he is with us. Very quietly we go on, knowing he has come; but like John we know we have to share this hope with others. Others need to be baptized into this waiting.

These moments of grace are not the end of our waiting. The mystery we enter through the waiting always points us beyond ourselves into the future. Only now our hearts are healed a little as we look to the future.

> As the people were in expectation, and all men questioned in their hearts concerning John, whether perhaps he was the Christ, John answered them all, "I baptize you with water; but he who is mightier than I is coming, the thong of whose sandals I am not worthy to untie; he will baptize you with the Holy Spirit and with fire"(Luke 3:15-16).

God found John as he waited in the wilderness and touched him. He became a man set apart who could awaken the deep hopes for God that slumbered in the hearts of men. But he knew he had to stay faithful to his waiting with and for God. His waiting was not yet finished. This is the deep humility that sometimes grows in a heart during years of waiting. Such a heart knows that waiting for God has its seasons. There is the waiting of early years that is often filled with great expectancy. There is another kind of waiting that is like being lost in a dark wood where we cannot find our way.

Waiting for God eventually brings us to boundary situations like death, the silence of God, or the collapse of our own vision of integrity. Then remembering our past is of no help for the Lord is dealing with me in a startlingly new way. He is drawing me into the dark wilderness of my own heart, across the personal geography of my own inner space. But this is uncharted. For me it is unexplored. It is a surprising, sometimes frightening landscape that constantly looks much different than I think it should, or from the way I would like it to be. Only faith lets me know that this is the way home, though it is not traveled by my own wits and assumptions. Here I learn to wait for the Lord, who alone sees the way.[2]

John seems to have entered into this dark wood at the hands of Herod.

> But Herod the tetrarch, who had been reproved by him for Herodias, his brother's wife, and for all the evil things that Herod had done, added this to them all, that he shut up John in prison (Luke 3:19-20).

John sits in prison waiting. The story seeps into me. Even after Jesus' coming, when he was in prison for speaking the truth, John was still waiting and wondering. My heart goes to the story in Luke 7:18-23 where John sends asking, "Are you the one?"

> The disciples of John told him of all these things. And John, calling to him two of his disciples, sent them to the Lord, saying, "Are you he who is to come, or shall we look for another?" And when the men had come to him, they said, "John the Baptist has sent us to you, saying, 'Are you he who is to come, or shall we look for another?' " In that hour he cured many of the diseases and plagues and evil spirits, and on many that were blind he bestowed sight. And he answered them, "Go and tell John what you have seen and heard: The blind receive their sight, the lame walk, lepers are cleansed, and the deaf hear, the dead are raised up, the poor have the good news preached to them. And blessed is he who takes no offense at me."

As I live this story I begin to know something of what was

happening in John. I stand here in the middle of my own life, imprisoned by my own selfishness and fears and in some ways by yours as well; and I find myself asking the same thing John did: "Is this it? Is this what I have been waiting for?" Jesus' response to John's question gnaws at me, especially the ending "Blessed is he who takes no offense at me." John already knows of Jesus' preaching and the healings he performs. What, then, is Jesus saying to John and to me? I begin to think it is a call to discern in these events what I had not seen. Before I entered this dark wood it was so easy to say that these were signs of the mystery of God's saving love. But now, as I pray over these words, I start to think that this probably wasn't quite what John was expecting. He seems to have been waiting for the heavens to be torn open and for this sinful age to come to a crashing end. Then God who had been silent for so long would come in power and glory bringing the new age, where the faithful would live in peace with him and one another. But what we have here, for all its miraculous power, is so ordinary, so everyday. What of all those who weren't touched by Jesus? A few people come to see. A few get fed. But power, as John knows, remains ruthless. Pilate and Herod still rule. The high priests are not men of faith. The world hasn't been ripped apart and put together in a healed way. The Prophet rots in prison while Jesus invites him to still believe. "Blessed is he who takes no offense at me." I see myself so clearly in John. I could go into the wilderness with hope that God would come into my life, transforming it and my world. Now in this dark wood where his presence is so confusing, I can see how one could give up waiting in faith. God's presence is so hidden, and the agony about me is so intense.

Knowing what is happening in my heart, Jesus calls me back to waiting. When I first entered the wilderness I lived on the word of God. I read it with an open heart, letting the images sink into me. This is the way we have been praying over the gospel stories. As this way of praying deepens in you and me, it becomes a central part of our lives. Here I meet the Lord, my Beloved, and I am brought to life. Here I am strengthened so that I can be faithful to my mission in life, to family and friends. At least at times there is a sense of God's presence in my life, and I need that. I can't afford to let it go. Then I find that this prayer is becoming more and more passive, more and more vague. Then it is gone, only to come back in flashes and be gone again. The silence takes over. I know I am losing my way of listening to the word of the Lord. This is very frightening. I feel the dark wood closing in on me.

It went in the past, but then the reasons were clear: I got tired of it. Boredom set in and I fell away. Or there was some kind of serious infidelity. But this does not seem to be the case here. Still, there is a sense in which I cannot pray the way I did, or at least not regularly. One day I can, but then for two or three days it just doesn't work anymore. Further, I experience this real disinclination to pray in this way, even though I am more serious about wanting to pray than ever before. Instead I feel drawn to sit before the tabernacle in silence. Welling up from the depths there is a need to be totally still and wait for God. An emptiness opens up before me. Unlike the filled quiet of my previous prayer, this stillness seems so empty.

This is a passage that happens differently for different people. For some, at first there are no words; the imagination stops; there is no thinking. Gradually there is a developing awareness that there isn't just silence either. In the very silence there is someone present, someone who stirs you up, who frightens you, who burns you. It isn't peace you find here, or at least not serenity, but painful excitement. Afterwards you have the feeling that you are more real and deeper and are drawn again the next day to meet this raging fire in the darkness that is beyond words. Gradually we come to sense that this is God, the Father of Jesus whom he brings us to meet; and we intuitively know it is so painful because he is really close to us and changing us. While the experience of prayer isn't easy, a great peace, a funda- mental integrity, tends to settle over the rest of our lives. We are more energetic in our work, more faithful in our commitments. Our lives seem more focused.

In the beginning of this new phase in prayer there often are no words, or if there are it means that we are distracted. However, for some people there comes a point when there is a word; and that word is uttered into the darkness in faith, into the darkness that might upset us, but that also calls to us with a strange healing joy. Usually such a word is short. "God." "Father." "Jesus." "Help." There is nothing more to say. That little word says it all. It says what I am or would be but cannot explain or act out or even understand. But in that word I collect myself and hurl myself into the searing but healing darkness. Meanwhile this still and holy darkness calls to me, purifies me, vivifies me. I say the word and then am still; then I say it again. These two ways of praying seem to be transitional; and as we grow into them, as the prayer deepens in us, they too gradually seem to be left behind. They seem to evaporate.

In God's wisdom he leads others directly into deep silence without any transition. Back when you could meditate you kind of knew you were praying. You could practically watch it. And in the silence dominated by God's holy presence there was a sense of awe, but at least there was no question that it was real. Now things become so vague. I sit down to pray. I read the gospel stories and then slip into this bland silence. It seems to come upon me. But is there anyone there? Is this just daydreaming? It is very hard to tell. Am I playing games?

There is a greater sense of detachment, a greater longing for God, and a desire, even an ability to follow Jesus in his way of simplicity, trust and service. And there is this perplexing silence into which I seem to be drawn. The fear is that there is no one there in the silence. This is a crucial turning point. Can I choose to wait in silence, to wait when I cannot understand what is happening, can hardly experience it? Do I intuitively trust the God who calls me into this stillness? Or do I panic when I can no longer understand, or experience God's presence? This is a passage of the spiritual life where the path of fidelity is to wait. To trust what God is doing, even when we can't understand it. After all where is our trust? In God or our own understanding and experience? The words of Eliot come back at me telling me what to do.

> I said to my soul, be still, and wait without hope
> For hope would be hope for the wrong thing;
> wait without love for love would be love of the wrong thing;
> there is yet faith but the faith and the love and
> the hope are all in the waiting.
> Wait without thought, for you are not ready for thought:
> So the darkness shall be the light, and the stillness the dancing.[3]

If we wait, slowly the stillness deepens. We have to let the words, the images, the more tangible sense of God go. God is moving in the depths of the heart, deeper than the intellect or imagination can reach. This takes time and patience and trust. There may come a time when the imagination can be wandering around upstairs, but you are silent below it. Because the prayer has moved deeper within us, to bother with this chatter that is going on upstairs would draw us away from the real encounter with God that is happening on a much deeper level. In the deepening silence, beyond words and images, beyond anything you or I can understand, any meaning that can be adequately expressed in words, God is forming us in the depths of our hearts. This is what Jeremiah has told us.[4]

> The word that came to Jeremiah from the Lord: "Arise and go down to the potter's house, and there I will let you hear my words." So I went down to the potter's house, and there he was working at his wheel. And the vessel he was making of clay was spoiled in the potter's hand, and he reworked it into another vessel, as it seemed good to the potter to do.
>
> Then the word of the Lord came to me: "O House of Israel, can I not do with you as this potter has done? says the Lord. Behold, like clay in the potter's hand, so are you in my hand, O House of Israel."
> (Jeremiah 18:1-6)

This learning to wait in a deeper way does not happen only in prayer. Often the facts of our lives draw us into situations where it is very hard to tell what is the path of fidelity. Reality becomes so complicated. With a simplicity that is really new we are willing to follow the Lord wherever he leads, but we can't see where that is. This is a time of pruning. We grope along being drawn into situations where there are few clear-cut answers. We find ourselves bound to others and the Lord in ways we hardly understand, that seem to lack the clarity of our early years in the wilderness. We can't guarantee what will happen tomorrow. The sure conviction that somehow "it will all work out" slips away from us. I am face to face with situations that seem to be dead ends. My old way of listening to the Lord, making decisions and trying to carry them through ruthlessly won't work any more. I have to learn to trust more deeply, waiting for the Lord to do what seems to be impossible. I cling to the words of Micah.

> He has showed you, O man, what is good
> and what does the Lord require of you
>   but to do justice, and love kindness,
> and to walk humbly with your God?
> (Micah 6:8)

In Luke 9:7-9 we hear very matter-of-factly that John has died in prison still waiting.

> Now Herod the tetrarch heard of all that was done, and he was perplexed, because it was said by some that John had been raised from the dead, by some that Elijah had appeared, and by others that one of the old prophets had risen. Herod said, "John I beheaded; but who is this about whom I hear such things?" And he sought to see him.

Humanly speaking it looks like nothing happened, that the waiting was a dead end. Back in Luke 7:26 Jesus had called John a prophet, "Yes, I tell you, and more than a prophet." To believe Jesus is to enter into another season of waiting, to open one's self up to waiting that is a kind of death. Sometimes this leads me to wait for my friends' lives to be healed. When I have done what I can, or while I continue to do it, I often have to wait in faith not pretending I understand. At other times I have to wait as a loved one dies or collapses before my eyes, when all I can do is wait as I agonize with them. There is nothing you can do, absolutely nothing, except be with the other in their pain and dependence. And our own helpless inadequacies and fumbling attempts to comfort confront us with our poverty. This is a desert that I never imagined, but here I am baptized into waiting. In the waiting our prayers change from, "Let this chalice pass us by," to "dear Lord, release him soon from this suffering" to "dear Lord, your will, your time, your place . . .whatever your heart dictates. Because even in, and perhaps especially in, pain and confusion we are enveloped in your love." After my prayer I think maybe one day I'll see clearly enough to strike that "perhaps" out of that last sentence.

And life goes on. In this killing waiting our illusions die. We are forced to face our utter poverty; we are drawn into a fidelity to the Lord and others deeper than we can understand. In this killing waiting the prophecy of Ezekiel begins to happen in my heart.

> A new heart I will give you, and a new spirit I will put within you; and I will take out of your flesh the heart of stone and give you a heart of flesh. And I will put my spirit within you, and cause you to walk in my statutes and be careful to observe my ordinances. You shall dwell in the land which I gave to your fathers; and you shall be my people, and I will be your God. (Ezekiel 36:26-28)

[1]Cf. W. Wink, *John the Baptist in the Gospel Tradition.* Cambridge, 1968.

[2]This seems to be very close to what John of the Cross counsels in *The Living Flame*, III, 29. "The soul, then should advert that God is the principal agent in this matter, and that He acts as the blind man's guide who must lead it by the hand to the place it does not know to reach (to supernatural things of which neither its intellect, will, nor memory can know the nature). It should use all its principal care in watching so as not to place any obstacle in the way of its guide on the road that God has ordained for it according to His law and of the faith, as we said."

[3]T.S. Eliot, *Four Quartets.* N.Y.: Harvest Books, 1971. These lines come from "East Coker," lines 122-127.

[4]For the classical analysis of this transition into silent prayer see John of the Cross, *The Ascent*, II, 12-15; *Dark Night*, I, 9-10 and *The Living Flame*, III, 32-49.

The Grain of Wheat

Years of listening to Jesus in the gospels slide by and one day it finally occurs to us that Jesus hardly ever gives a straight answer. He is always inviting people into the Kingdom; but when someone finally asks him, "What is this Kingdom you are always talking about?" we see him pause. He thinks for a moment and says, "Well, it's like a man who had two sons . . .," or "It's like a man who was blind and who was given his sight." Jesus is always telling stories, suggesting images that hint at more than can be said. As I notice this I start to picture the response of people. I can see some of them stop short, knowing there is something there in the image or the parable, though they can't say what it is. Quietly they open their hearts to what Jesus has said and they go away pondering it. I see them going back to it year after year, "The Kingdom is like a man in search of fine pearls . . ." Gradually this changes their hearts. The reality of the Kingdom starts to seep into their lives as they live within the story. Years later someone, seeing something of the depth that had grown in them, might ask them, "What happened to you?" They would pause, think for a moment and say, "Well, it's like a man who had two sons . . ."

In John 12:24 Jesus uses one of these images to speak of his death.

Truly, truly, I say to you, unless a grain of wheat falls to the ground and dies, it remains alone; but if it dies, it bears much fruit.

I know that it is time to take this image into my heart and let it work on me, but I'm afraid. I just don't want to open my heart to the confusion, the pain, the dying. I try to hide from it, but I can't. After days of putting it off, somewhere deep inside me I finally give in and I am at peace.

I sit down and open the gospels. "Unless a grain of wheat falls into the ground and dies . . ." I feel myself falling, disoriented. My world is slipping away from me, and much that was so important seems unreal. My work that seemed so important, I leave it behind. It is gone. My hopes that I could make something of myself, they, too, are gone. My plans! I've always been making plans, planning what I would finish today, what I would tackle next month. Now, it's hard to tell why that seemed so important. I experience them drying up before my eyes. I'm left without things to do, things to achieve. I look for those I love. They can't touch me. I seem to be falling beyond the reach of their loving care. Nor can I get back to them. I still hold them in my heart, but something is gone. I can't quite make out what it is. The words come to me, "It's over, done."

The world goes on; but I won't. What will happen to those I love? I don't know. Terribly aware of their needs and fragility, I have to let them go. What will happen to me? Again, I don't know. I have to entrust those I love and myself to the Father, and here there is no longer any room for pretense. Faced with my own collapsing limits I either trust the Father unconditionally or I panic. The terror that we are all alone in the universe comes back to me, and I am defenseless before it. Then the Father's love touches my heart and I give it back to him; I know he is there and will save me. Here my surrender is without affectation; there is nothing I can give him, no achievement I can hide behind. I'm stripped and exposed but not unloved.

Dimly I had thought that this would be ravaging. Instead I find it is just numbing. I really don't understand. I don't even try to. I sit here stunned, confused, but trusting. In this numbed silence I look to the crucifix.[1] My heart tries to embrace the Crucified One, as never before. With crystal clarity I see Jesus. He is what I have always needed to be: the Beloved of God, the Guiltless One, trusting, totally simple, a man for others. Now I see that because he was all of that without reservation or apology he had to die. In a rush of confusion and resentment I see what I have never let myself see: that he had to die for me. I had to kill him. He is so clearly what I desperately need to be but have always been blocked from being. In the depth of my heart I have never fully believed I was the Father's beloved; there has always been the brooding ground of guilt in me. The roots of my selfishness have blocked my simplicity and trust. Flooded by all of this, that I have spent years trying to leave behind as I journeyed with Jesus, I lash out at what I'm not. The deep reservoirs of my fear and guilt break over me as I stand before Pilate and beneath the cross screaming in rage. I kill him.

I can't bear him, and yet I love him. Caught off guard and overwhelmed by this explosion that has brought to the surface the roots of my sinfulness, I cannot believe that the Father could love me.[2] Not while I kill his Beloved Son. My dark side takes over, and I embrace it even while I hate it and myself. I find myself cut off, isolated. My fear and resentment distort my heart turning me against others, God and myself. I'm trapped. I live the isolation of the grain of wheat that refuses to die. I'm sterile. I remember my past fidelities, the years of faithful prayer, my journeys with Jesus through different wildernesses, my growing ability to serve and be simple. Now it all rings hollow. Others might be gradually healed by God's love in this way, but the true state of my heart has been revealed in this outburst. I see clearly the dark underside of my past fidelity. It was self-serving. In the midst of all this I would cry out to the Lord for help, but I open my heart and I cannot speak. I'm paralyzed. I am being killed by the same terror that rose up in me to kill Jesus.

I look back to the Crucified One and see that even in his agony and death his arms are out to embrace me. My heart dissolves. Welling up out of me come the words of the centurion, "Truly this man was the Son of God!" (Mk. 15:39). This is the great pouring out of God's love. Only the Crucified One can reveal to me the depth of human darkness, my darkness, and the extent to which God embraces it, embraces me. I had fled from the cross, hidden from it any way I could. Here inside this image of the grain of wheat, I find that my only safety is clinging to the Crucified One.

> If anyone serves me, he must follow me; and where I am, there shall my servant be also . . . (John 12:26).

This had sounded like a dreadful challenge, now it is my only hope.

---

[1]Readers of Sebastian Moore's *The Crucified Jesus Is No Stranger*. N.Y.: Seabury, 1977, will be able to see how deeply I have been influenced by that book, even though I do not quote it here.

[2]This has certain similarities with what John of the Cross calls the dark night of spirit passive. See *Dark Night*, II, 4-8.

Resurrection

The reality of God's love for us is revealed in Christ crucified, dead, and risen. Living within the image of the grain of wheat opens up our hearts to the Crucified One; the resurrection stories close the circle. Here we meet the Risen One and are assimilated to him.[1] Our hearts are once again transformed as we are drawn into the One who is the Beloved of the Father and who loves the Father in return. This knowing and being known, this loving and being loved brings us home, for this is our true destiny. This seems to be something of what Jesus had in mind when he prayed:

> I do not pray for these only, but also for those who believe in me through their word, that they may all be one; even as thou, Father, art in me, and I in thee, that they also may be in us, so that the world may believe that thou hast sent me. The glory which thou hast given me I have given to them, that they may be one even as we are one, I in them and thou in me, that they may be perfectly one, so that the world may know that thou hast sent me and hast loved them even as thou hast loved me.
> (John 17:20-23)

Coming from long days of living within the image of the grain of wheat that brings the shadow of the cross into my very being, it seems very easy to understand something of what was going on inside the hearts of the disciples as they hid together in the upper room.

On the evening of that day, the first day of the week, the door being shut where the disciples were, for fear of the Jews, Jesus came and stood among them and said to them, "Peace be with you." When he had said this, he showed them his hands and his side. Then the disciples were glad when they saw the Lord. Jesus said to them again, "Peace be with you. As the Father has sent me, even so I send you." And when he had said this, he breathed on them, and said to them, "Receive the Holy Spirit. If you forgive the sins of any, they are forgiven; if you retain the sins of any, they are retained" (John 20:19-23).

I can feel their fear and the heavy sense of betrayal that suffocated them. Their hopes are all gone. The power of darkness has conquered and now it is devouring their souls. Then, the unspeakable! He is present in their midst. "Peace be with you." The terror is displaced by hope, by the presence of what I had given up hoping for. He knows my fears. He reads through my betrayal. He shows me the scars that betrayal brought him, but there is no accusation. "Peace be with you." He embraces my whirling heart. The spirit of his victory and compassion floods into me and I come alive. Then, he sends me.

This is almost too good to be true. As a matter of fact this is Thomas' reaction.

Now Thomas one of the twelve, called the twin, was not with them when Jesus came. So the other disciples told him, "We have seen the Lord." But he said to them, "Unless I see in his hands the print of the nails, and place my finger in the mark of the nails, and place my hand in his side, I will not believe." (John 20:24-25)

How I know this Thomas. There is a refreshing bluntness to his scepticism. He has seen too many dead bodies to believe just because the others say so. Who knows, perhaps they are cracking up. This echoes in my heart bringing to the fore my own doubts. I read the gospel stories. My hopes flare up.

My heart is moved, then somehow the old doubts come back. I can see much of myself in this man who won't pretend he believes. My terror and guilt seem to be so deep that it is hard to break them once and for all. In the meantime I can use Thomas as my model. He did not abandon the community of believers just because he had doubts. He stayed with them because he knew that only Jesus could heal his heart, if only . . .if only it all were true. Eight days later he came to see, the doubts that had tortured him were dispelled by the presence of the Risen One. "My Lord and my God." This was the decisive turning point in Thomas' life. He was freed from the doubts that had always strangled him. Knowing how my own doubts ravage my heart and longing to really believe, I can sense how such a coming to faith would be like being freed from the bonds of death. It would be like a resurrection.

Stepping into this story with Thomas I discover two things. If only the presence of the Risen One can free me of these killing doubts, then I must stay in the community of faith, patiently waiting for the Lord, but waiting for him inside the resurrection stories. If I open up my heart to Peter and Mary Magdalen and their meetings with the Risen One perhaps I, too, can meet him and experience something of the power of his resurrection in my heart. Secondly, the existence into which Jesus entered with his resurrection is beyond words; but I can see something of it as it touched Thomas. It is a world where doubts no longer kill us. As I see how this healed Peter and Mary perhaps the reality of the resurrection will seem less vague and the Lord will be able to use this to draw me into his new life.

But Mary stood weeping outside the tomb, and as she wept she stooped to look into the tomb; and she saw two angels in white, sitting where the body of Jesus had lain, one at the head and

one at the feet. They said to her, "Woman, why are you
weeping?" She said to them, "Because they have taken away my
Lord, and I do not know where they have laid him." Saying this,
she turned around and saw Jesus standing, but she did not
know that it was Jesus. Jesus said to her, "Woman, why are you
weeping? Whom do you seek?" Supposing him to be the
gardener, she said to him, "Sir, if you have carried him away,
tell me where you have laid him, and I will take him away."
Jesus said to her, "Mary." She turned and said to him in
Hebrew, "Rabboni!" (which means Teacher). Jesus said to her,
"Do not hold me, for I have not yet ascended to the Father; but
go to my brethren and say to them, I am ascending to my
Father and your Father, to my God and your God."
(John 20:11-17)

My own doubts draw me into Mary's terrors. Like Mary I
have journeyed with Jesus. He has saved me from a grubby
life of chaos and despair. He has given me hope. He has
understood me and loved me as no one else. Then he's
gone, murdered by the fear and selfishness, the resentment
that he had embraced in me. Now the terror that I am all
alone after all wells up inside me. If Jesus can't break this
annihilating isolation I'm doomed. I can't even find his
body. This man asks me why I'm weeping, who it is I want.
I'm weeping from despair and loss. I tremble with terror. I
search in utter desperation for the One my heart loves.
Years ago my troubled scattered heart sought many things.
Now it is him alone. But he is gone, killed, and the new life
he had begun in me is collapsing.

   Then I hear him calling me by name, that special name
that lets me know how he treasures me. In the story it is
"Mary" but as I turn this over in my heart again and again I
hear my own name. I know the Risen One is there, that he
wants me; and my heart is drawn out of the terror of death.
I'm not alone. He is with me. Healed by this I am sent to
share this new life with my brothers and sisters. What is this

resurrected life like? It's hard to say. What exactly is the Risen One like? I have no words. But after he has touched me, the terror that I am alone is gone. I feel like I am alive for the first time. My previous life now looks like a kind of death. Here I discover that whatever else happened to Jesus at his resurrection, he seems to have entered into a way of being where terror cannot reach; and as I live in this story that way of living is even now beginning in me.

Peter's meeting with the Risen Lord was somewhat different. He had pledged himself to Jesus, then betrayed him. This haunted Peter. Added to the collapse of his hopes was the crushing burden of his denials.

> When they had finished breakfast, Jesus said to Simon Peter, "Simon, son of John, do you love me more than these?" He said to him, "Yes, Lord; you know that I love you." He said to him, "Feed my lambs." A second time he said to him, "Simon, son of John, do you love me?" He said to him, "Yes, Lord; you know that I love you." He said to him, "Tend my sheep." He said to him the third time, "Simon, son of John, do you love me?" Peter was grieved because he said to him the third time, "Do you love me?" And he said to him, "Lord, you know everything; you know that I love you." Jesus said to him, "Feed my sheep. Truly, truly, I say to you, when you were young, you girded yourself and walked where you would; but when you are old, you will stretch out your hands, and another will gird you and carry you where you do not wish to go." (This he said to show by what death he was to glorify God). And after this he said to him, "Follow me" (John 21:15-19).

Many things stir in Peter's heart. He is overjoyed to see Jesus. But he is also unsure. His betrayal eats at him. These last days, days of fear, betrayal, defeat, and overwhelming isolation, have changed Peter. The brashness is gone. He is painfully aware of his limits. The awful possibilities of the human heart are well known to him. Finally, Jesus turns to him, turns to me: "Do you love me?" In the past I said "Yes" so quickly, with such easy and unjustified confidence. Now, it is so hard to tell, except that these days have stripped me and forced me to see that if there is anyone I love it is Jesus. "Yes, Lord; you know that I love you." Then, he sends me to share this with others: "Feed my lambs." Again the same question, and a third time. This is killing. Three questions for three denials. My shame is exposed. My dark side gently but firmly brought into the light. He forces me to act it out. But this is reconciliation, not accusation. He embraces me in my deepest sinfulness. What I have always hidden from in myself he accepts. What I have always feared and hated he is willing to face. He loves me anyhow. As he embraces me in my utter vulnerability the gnawing suspicion that I am unlovable dissolves. He sees right through me. I no longer have to pretend and hide; he loves me just as I am. He still chooses me. He sends me to care for his flock. A weight is lifted. I sob in quiet, thankful peace. I don't have to pretend anymore. He loves me clear through. This is a resurrection.

To really be touched by the Risen One is like awakening from a nightmare of fear and guilt and unending loneliness. It is like coming back from the dead. Here we begin to know what the resurrection means, for it has already begun in us. We begin to understand something of what Jesus was talking about when he said:

> I am the resurrection and the life; he who believes in me, though he die, yet shall he live, and whoever lives and believes in me shall never die (John 11:25-26).

---

[1]For background on the Resurrection stories see R.H. Fuller, *The Formation of the Resurrection Narratives.* N.Y.: Macmillan, 1971.

A Non-Systematic Postscript

For most of us our religious lives began with intuitive impressions and responses. We glimpsed our vulnerability; we somehow were brought to trust an awesome presence that seemed to surround us and support us. These deep flashes of our childhood were connected with the silence of the church on Sunday morning, the presence of parents, the stories we were told about Jesus. The experiences were intense but without words. The connections with church and family and Jesus gave us simple ways of understanding something of what was happening to us.

Later years gave us an avalanche of words. Our catechism study filled our heads with definitions and precise summaries of long and complicated developments. Jesus was the second person of the Trinity, two natures in one God. The Church was...sacraments were... This information was duly tucked away. We accepted it as true, as terribly important. But the exact connection of all of this to what happened when I went to mass, or what my heart experienced when I said my prayers, was hazy. Surprisingly, I hardly realized how hazy it was. I believed; I said my prayers; I was accustomed to live with what could not be understood.

Praying within the Gospel stories can give me a new experience of Jesus and of myself, as well as a new way of thinking about those experiences. Jesus is the one who knows how to pray. He is the Beloved of the Father, the Guiltless One. He is the one who gives away his life for me. He is the Risen One. I am the one who will never be at peace until I, too, like Jesus, am the beloved of the Father. I am the one being healed of my blindness, called to wait, to be pure of heart. This starts to put new life into the answers I memorized as a child. To say that Jesus is the Beloved Son of the Father is to see the real meaning behind the statement that he is the second person of the Trinity. To experience how Jesus calls me with the very voice of God at the same time that I see him walking the hills of Galilee is to transform the words "one person in two natures" from intellectual furniture of the mind into knowledge of the heart. To speak of transforming the facts of our lives into mysteries opens up to us a new way of looking at the sacraments and our whole life in the church. The experiences we live and the religious language we speak start to converge and our lives become more integrated. This can be a great help.

With good cause someone might ask: "But what of the Spirit?" The early Christians came to see that Jesus was divine, but that he was not the Father. After all Jesus had not been praying to himself. The history of this development is complicated,[1] but one of the central convictions that emerged from it was the insight that in his human life Jesus lived out that which constituted the eternal relationship of the Son to the Father. As a man, everything he did, everything he was, was a translation into human terms, not just of divinity, but of the divinity of the Son; so it was the divinity that was derived, received. How was that lived out in a human way? Through Jesus' acceptance of the uncon- ditional love of his Father, the living of a life that was pure gift, as what was given by the Father. This resulted in his making manifest the true nature of the Father. "He who has seen me has seen the Father" (Jn. 14:9). Of course, the complement of his receiving his being from the Father was his turning to the Father in love, in obedience, in prayer, in purity of heart. "My food is to do the will of him who sent me" (Jn. 4:34).

This acting out of sonship was pushed to an extreme in Jesus' death on the cross. In a very real way the man from Nazareth became his act of trust in the Father, became the Son's love for the Father in human form, total, whole, complete. Even in the flesh he was that relationship to the Father. With the resurrection the unrestrained giving that was the Father's relationship to his son flooded even into the flesh of Jesus. Gradually the Christian tradition came to see that this reciprocal relationship of love between the Father and the Son is the Holy Spirit. That reciprocal relationship of unconditional acceptance and purity of heart, which is the Holy Spirit, was unleashed on the world at the resurrection. The Risen One became the sender of the Spirit, and it is the gift of the spirit of God's love poured into our hearts (Rom. 5:5) that calls us to give our hearts to this Jesus. The Spirit, then, has been in our hearts drawing us to hope, to trust, to follow Jesus. He has been there prodding us, breaking down the barriers of fear and guilt that keep us back from our true home, the interior life of God where Father and Son and Spirit are one.

---

[1]For the scriptural development see Fuller, *The Foundations of New Testament Christology.* N.Y.: Scribners, 1965; for the patristic and early conciliar development see A. Grillmeir, *Christ in Christian Tradition.* London: Mowbray and Co., 1964.

Other Titles from St. Bede's

WORD & SPIRIT, a monastic review published once a year. Bringing together the work of international scholars, it offers important insights in its conspectus of man's remarkable religious heritage:

No. 1, 1979 — dedicated to St. Basil the Great. Articles by Jean Gribomont, Adalbert de Vogüé, Jean Daniélou, Basil Pennington and others.

No. 2, 1980 — in honor of the 1500th anniversary of the birth of St. Benedict. Articles by Jean Leclercq, Hans Urs von Balthasar, Hubert van Zeller, André Louf, and others.

No. 3, 1981 — to commemorate the 1600th anniversary of Constantinople I, on the Holy Spirit and on Prayer. Articles by Julian Stead, Jordan Aumann, Hans Urs von Balthasar and others. *To be published in Summer 1981.*

Finding Grace at the Center, *Pennington, Keating and Clarke*. This book is an introduction to the centering prayer by an abbot and two priests—each well-qualified to present his subject, exploring different aspects of the centering prayer.

Crisis of Faith, *Thomas Keating, OCSO*. Keating teaches you to take your trials in stride using the gospel to guide you.

Centered on Christ, *Augustine Roberts, OCSO*. The book's evolution reveals its specifically monastic roots: it began as Thomas Merton's mimeographed notes on the vows, was revised by Roberts in the light of the changing theological climate generated by Vatican II.

Song of a Happy Man, *Anselm Fitzgerald, O.C.S.O.* Father Anselm, a Trappist monk, gives us a delightful example of the maxim that prayer is a conversation with God. Inspired by Psalm 91, he shares his prayers, sighs, memories and thoughts with our loving Father.

The Rule of Peace, *Christopher Derrick*. Discusses the relevance of monasticism in today's world and even the need for it. Derrick presents St. Benedict's *Rule* as a remedy for the problems we all face today.

St. Sharbel, *Claire M. Benedict*. The wonder-working attributed to St. Sharbel gives hope that, out of the tragedy that is present-day Lebanon, true healing will come by union with Christ.

Rafka, *Bishop Francis M. Zayek*. Deals beautifully with the problem of suffering. Rafka's search for her ultimate vocation—generous and wholehearted love—has merited for her the pending beatification of the Church.

Order from:
St. Bede's Publications
Box 132
Still River, Massachusetts 01467